TALKING SAFETY

*For the wonderful couple, married 56 years now,
that my children call Nanny Babs and Grandad*

Talking Safety

A User's Guide to World Class Safety Conversation

Second Edition

Dr Tim Marsh

GOWER

Published by
Gower Publishing Limited
Wey Court East
Union Road
Farnham
Surrey GU9 7PT
England

Gower Publishing Company
110 Cherry Street
Suite 3-1
Burlington, VT 05401-3818
USA

www.gowerpublishing.com

British Library Cataloguing in Publication Data
Marsh, Tim, Dr.
  Talking safety : a user's guide to world class safety
  conversation. -- 2nd ed.
  1. Industrial safety.
  I. Title
  658.4'08-dc23

The Library of Congress has cataloged the printed edition as follows:
Marsh, Tim (Psychologist)
  Talking safety : a user's guide to world class safety conversation / by Tim Marsh.
      pages cm
  Includes bibliographical references and index.
  ISBN 978-1-4094-6655-0 (pbk) -- ISBN 978-1-4094-6656-7 (ebook) -- ISBN 978-1-4094-6657-4 (epub) 1. Industrial safety. 2. Personnel management. I. Title.
  T55.M3558 2013
  658.3'82--dc23
                                                              2013001177

9781409466550 (pbk)
9781409466567 (ebk – PDF)
9781409466574 (ebk – ePUB)

Printed and bound in Great Britain
by MPG PRINTGROUP

Contents

List of Figures

About the Author

Tim Marsh was one of the team leaders of the original UK research into behavioural safety in the early 1990s and is a Chartered Psychologist and a Chartered Fellow of IOSH. He has worked with more than 400 organisations around the world since including the European Space Agency and the BBC. He now specialises in safety leadership and organisational culture assessment and change. Tim runs open courses on Behavioural Safety and Safety Culture for IOSH, was awarded a 'President's Commendation' in 2008 by the International Institute of Risk and Safety Management and was selected to be their first ever 'Specialist Fellow' in 2010. The author of several bestselling books Tim is a regular contributor to magazines including the *Safety and Health Practitioner* and *Health and Safety at Work*. Tim has a reputation as a lively and engaging speaker and has presented at dozens of conferences around the world. In 2013 he was invited to give the key note 'Warner Address' at the 60th BOHS International Conference.

Ryder Marsh Safety Limited can be contacted via their website: www.rydermarsh.co.uk.

ACKNOWLEDGEMENTS

Professor Neil Budworth who's comments on the first edition of this book were invaluable, and to Jonathan Norman of Gower who's comments on this edition were equally helpful and constructive.

With many thanks to Roger Beale for providing the fantastic cartoons for this book.

Preface

This book is intended as a response to feedback about my first book. It is a stand-alone piece for the number of readers whose view is:

> *A standard safety leadership book of 200 reasonably concise pages with a few nice cartoons is all very well but I could do with something that is more concise and tells me exactly what to do for 'a first step'? Minimum theory, no options, just what to do for the first step … what do we do if we don't do anything else?*

The good news is that, as ever, the 80:20 principle does apply and if you only do 'step one' *well* you'll achieve the fabled step change of a 50 per cent reduction in accidents with this alone. I absolutely *guarantee* it.

There has to be a little theory for background I'm afraid – no one will do anything if you don't explain 'why' as well as 'what' – but I've aimed to keep that as concise as possible.

TWO STORIES BY WAY OF INTRODUCTION

If you'll allow me a little indulgence before the off I'd like to start with two stories to introduce myself and the book. Both *entirely* true.

The first refers to a Welsh rugby legend, Bobby Windsor, who was a neighbour of mine in South Wales. Indeed my father who was a teacher taught him at school. Bobby was part of the famous Pontypool front row that toured South Africa successfully in 1974. A series win!

In those days there were no mobile phones, of course, and a team meeting was called to sort out the problem of someone continually sneaking into the management's rooms to make phone calls home.

The management got the squad together and offered the offender the chance to confess.

Nothing.

They pointed out that all the calls were to the same number and that it was a *Pontypool* number ...

At which Bobby leapt to his feet and shouted 'Right! Which one of you bastards has been phoning my wife!?'

The Moral: There are times when you've taken a risk when you'll need to think on your feet.

The second story is about my Aunt Shirley who was pulled over for speeding by a young PC. He asked to see her driving licence but she said she didn't have one.

He asked if it was even her car that she was driving, but she said 'no it belonged to a Tom Jukes'. She was asked if Mr Jukes had lent her the car and she said that no, she'd stolen it, but only after she'd killed Tom, chopped him up and put him in the boot.

Shaken, the young PC called for back up and presently a senior officer arrived and took charge of the situation. 'Please step to the boot and open it madam' he said. My aunt did so. The boot was empty.

'Interesting ...' he said, and then asked, 'Could I see your driver's licence please?' and she said 'certainly' and handed it over. 'Is this your car?' he asked. 'Yes officer. Would you like to see the log book?' she smiled.

'No need for that', said the officer, 'but this is really very interesting. My young officer over there told me that you don't have a driving licence and that this isn't your car. Indeed he says that you stole this car from a Mr Tom Jukes who indeed, you'd killed, chopped up and put in the boot here'.

My aunt's response: 'Oh the lying little bugger! I bet he's only gone and told you I was *speeding* as well!'

The Moral: As above, if you are going to take risks at least keep your wits about you.

AND YOUR POINT IS?! YOU MAY WELL ASK ...

You may be thinking that these two so-called 'learning points' can't possibly underpin a safety book and you'd be right of course. As ever with a psychologist you just can't trust them and there's a hidden agenda.

What I've tried to do here are the following three things:

- To amuse you. (Simply because if you're smiling that's a good thing in itself. Life is too short is it not?)

- But also to surprise you pleasantly and try to get you thinking 'well this is going a lot better than I thought it would so far!'

- Because most importantly ... 'Step 1' of a safety talk, as below, is to 'Introduce yourself, break the ice and set the right tone' and I've tried in my own fashion to 'model' that here.

Introduction

This book is divided into two relatively short sections. The first section addresses the reasons why so many organisations undertake some form of 'walk and talk' process. It summarises the most recent thinking and innovation but assumes no prior knowledge and covers first principles. This because experience shows that a lot of people who have undertaken these safety conversations for years haven't had this explained to them!

It covers:

- why compliance is only half the story;

- why day-to-day behaviour is so important;

- why 'try harder and take more care' doesn't work;

- what world class safety leadership looks like *generally*.

Its basic aim is to establish why a dedicated walk and talk is so important to developing a strong safety culture and therefore in minimising the amount of unsafe behaviour.

With that covered the second section addresses, in the light of these theories and principles, the practicalities of what a really good conversation looks like. The suggested model contains just the five steps, which are:

- Introduce Yourself, Breaking the Ice and Setting the Tone.

- Objective Analysis and Learning.

- Coaching.

- Eliciting a Promise?

- Closing Out.

Where it seemed appropriate there are some practical lists in the background section and some background in the practical section. The aim is to make the book as logical and user friendly as it can be.

Before we start I'd like to tell you another story – this one illustrating perfectly the sort of dedication I so often see in the safety community and the obstacles it faces. I attended a key kick-off meeting with a safety professional who didn't seem his usual enthusiastic self. I'll call him Ian Morgan. As we chatted away waiting for the board to join us (they were late) he explained that he was having a bad day. A very bad day actually as he explained that he'd actually buried his father that morning. I was staggered and asked 'what on earth are you doing here?' but he simply said 'I know … but this session is really important'.

I found this really humbling and it reminded me that whilst the *devil* can certainly be in the detail of a simple conversation or act – so too can *inspiration*. Ian Whittingham MBE used

2

to describe the aftermath of the fall that paralysed him to remind us that the impact of events ripple out like dropping a stone in a pond. This works for positive events too. When I feel I'm banging my head against a wall of 'impressive words, less impressive action' I think of Ian Morgan and the others like him I've been lucky enough to meet.

I remind myself that every single good safety conversation sends out good ripples and is a brick in the wall of a strong safety culture.

Tim Marsh

A Little Theory

① Why Bother?

In this chapter I will cover:

- The limitations of compliance.

- The vital importance of day-to-day behaviour.

- Why you can't change behaviour with exhortations to 'Have a Good Attitude' in the medium to long term.

- The vital importance of Heinrich's Triangle and how it relates to behaviour and process safety.

WHY BOTHER?

If you've been given this book to read you may be asking 'why do we need this?' After all the company has some lovely certificates on the reception wall that are clear proof that you've passed some impressive sounding safety audits.

On the other hand, even if your organisation is broadly compliant and accident rates are at their best ever levels historically they've plateaued over the past few years and are nowhere near best in class (as is a key strategic aim) and senior management are determined that they *will* improve.

Sometimes this is the consequence of a serious incident and sometimes because senior management have been proactively convinced that good safety is good business – as in 'if you think safety is expensive try having an accident'.

Leaving aside the moral argument, excellent safety also has the spin-off benefits of enhanced reputation, improved morale and minimised disruption. More than that, to get to truly world class safety performance *inevitably* requires the embedding of a set of generic day-to-day behaviours whose effectiveness will generalise to everything from environment and health to quality and productivity.

Genuine safety excellence requires far more than good systems. It requires an on-going, day-to-day commitment to intelligent analysis and constructive communication. No organisation that genuinely embeds these behaviours as part of 'the way we do things around here' can possibly fail to derive all sorts of spin-off benefits.

THE LIMITATIONS OF COMPLIANCE

Many organisations reach a level of systems compliance that will please an auditing body and as above lead to lots of nice certificates in the lobby. These are of course very reassuring at a glance.

However, the observation that in the field 'compliance is *discretionary*' is absolutely true and underpins much of the rationale behind this book. More importantly, basic compliance simply isn't sufficient if you want to achieve any sort of *excellence* because research suggests that there is a better correlation between workforce *involvement* in safety and incident rate and *compliance* and incident rate.

If that sounds intuitively dubious please consider this question. Would you prefer your 10-year-old to simply step into the road blindly at a level crossing because the green 'walk' sign has come on or would you prefer them to cross 50 yards down the road whilst at the same time 'dynamic risk assessing' effectively as they go?

Companies like Premier Foods have recently been running much-lauded and award-winning safety campaigns where the emphasis is on fewer but *better* rules that are easier to enforce consistently and fairly. They are actively seeking to get away from compliance as an 'end in itself' and promote more *thinking* and *empowerment* in a search for genuine excellence.

What this means is that even if our employees actually do follow all the rules then we are still likely to be some way short of excellence. That's of course hypothetical because they *don't* always follow the rules. (To be honest no senior person in the safety culture field pays much attention at all to the certificates and awards in the foyer that the various auditing organisations deliver. At least not unless they aren't there *at all* of course!)

Recently the expressions 'operational discipline' and 'operating dexterity' have become much in vogue. What they mean in simple terms is thinking intelligently, imaginatively and flexibly around a solid foundation of controls.

It should all start with a focus on everyday behaviour.

THE VITAL IMPORTANCE OF BEHAVIOUR

There are two reasons why a behavioural focus is vital.

UNSAFE DAY-TO-DAY BEHAVIOUR CORRELATES WITH LOSS

There is always a direct link between the number of unsafe acts and the number of accidents. Heinrich's original triangle (see Figure 1.1) suggested that there are on average 300 unsafe acts per accident and the most recent HSE figures suggest two million unsafe behaviours per fatality. Arguing over the *exact* levels in the ratio doesn't matter; the simple fact is that there is a ratio. On balance we hurt many more people than we kill and we usually get away with a wide range of unsafe behaviours.

Usually.

For example, if the true likelihood of falling down the stairs of a building is 100,000 to 1 but one million people use the stairs annually – with none of them holding the handrail – then you'll have 10 accidents a year (give or take). If 90 per cent comply then there would be only one accident a year on average, but if we can get 99 per cent to comply then there would be only one accident every ten years or so – and 'zero accidents' becomes a possibility.

It's a simple numbers game.

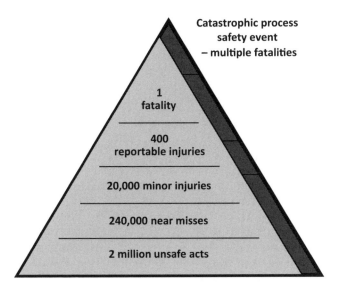

Figure 1.1   Occupational and process safety

Source: Adapted from H.W. Heinrich, 1959.

Notes: Attempts to show different triangles for process safety and personal safety suggest that the two are separate. Treating them as such is highly likely to be unproductive as several infamous case studies have shown. Although the outcomes can be different (EG injury on the one hand, loss of containment on the other) and the potential severity greater with an outright process failure they should be treated as different symptoms of the same root causes.

Heinrich's principle and gravity

This principle is important since for most companies the majority of accidents will be the result of simple slips, trips, falls and 'struck bys', so although excellent process safety is of course utterly vital to ensure something catastrophic doesn't happen, it's virtually impossible to have world class safety figures without a behavioural approach.

The staircase example above is illustrative as the majority of accidents have gravity as the root cause and however sophisticated our systems we can't design out gravity if we want to move our product or our people. (Think of any famous people who've been in the media following an accident. It's difficult to find anywhere the word 'fall' isn't involved; from the tragic death of actress Natasha Richardson after a fall on a nursery ski slope, to Ozzie Osborne falling off a quad bike and Keith Richards falling from a coconut tree.)

Even call centre employees will have to climb stairs and for many giant utility companies the single biggest cause of accidents is retail staff tripping over in the street walking from house to house and trying to update their palmtops as they go. (Two interesting facts: one, about 10 times as many people are killed each year by falling coconuts as by sharks with the numbers usually around 20:200. Two, more people have been killed erecting wind farms than by nuclear accidents.)

Because unsafe behaviours very rarely result in a near miss (let alone anything more serious) it's easy to assume they never will and forget Heinrich's principle. But here's a simple example to bear in mind. The first sunny weekend in spring in the UK will see lots of children bouncing around on trampolines all day and many of them will be unguarded. By the end of the day, *inevitably*, a handful will have suffered what are called 'life changing' injuries. I just can't tell you their names yet.

It's a simple numbers game; the bigger the number at the bottom of the triangle the bigger the number at the top will be. More positively, the opposite is also true. The smaller the number at the bottom of the triangle then the smaller the top number will be. This time, of course, we'll *never* know the names of those saved.

BEHAVIOUR SETS THE TONE AND IS SELF-REINFORCING

The second reason is that the very best definition of safety culture is 'the way we typically do things around here'. As in all walks of life a handful of key behaviours will set the tone and the first thing we do in a new situation is to look about and 'check out what's what'. If we see half the 'regulars' acting safely and half unsafely then as a new starter or subcontractor we can do pretty much what we want and not stand out. However, if we can improve these key behaviours so that 90 per cent comply (the fabled 'tipping point') then these behaviours become self-sustaining.

These key behaviours will range from the simple 'hold the handrail', 'look where you're walking' and 'using PPE' as above, through to the quality of a tool box talk, or perhaps an MD who closes out a strategy meeting that discussed cost-cutting with an aggressive 'any problems with that!? No? Good! Get on with it then ...'

Behaviour and peer pressure

The latest studies suggest that 80 per cent of what we learn is from our peers – only 5 per cent from formal training.

Imagine arriving in a new country and being told by the hire car people 'we're brutal with speeding on this island ... don't even think about exceeding 100kph'; reinforced with huge threatening signs as you drive out of the airport. You'd very probably join the motorway at 95kph, but you find in practice that the inside lane is averaging 100, the middle 120 and the outside lane is a complete free for all. What speed would you be doing five minutes later? (At conferences on the back of a number of 'well you have to keep up with flow for safety' comments I've started asking 'how many of us would have used the *outside lane* within half an hour?' Interestingly it's always about 50 per cent!)

So ... vision statements and company values are vital of course in setting the tone but they are the very definition of 'necessary but not *sufficient*'. They (should!) certainly *influence* the culture but they are not *it*. The day-to-day behaviour is – and it is almost impossible to overstate its importance.

YOU CAN'T ADDRESS BEHAVIOUR BY EXHORTING 'HAVE A GOOD ATTITUDE!'

Just about every study shows that 50 per cent of us think we have an average attitude and 50 per cent a *good* attitude (I exaggerate, but only a little – the actual figures from a Scottish driving study are about 48 per cent and 49 per cent). So when we talk about people who cut corners and take risks and say 'you know who you are!', the entire audience will point to the person next to them saying 'they're talking about you'. We all know people with a poor attitude of course but it's almost never the person in the mirror. And because there's nothing wrong with our attitudes thank you very much we don't need to change them ... I mean have you ever won an argument about sport, politics or religion? Ever? Have you changed an attitude about any of those subjects in the last 20 years?

Inspirational speakers can help get through this denial in the *short term* just as new football managers can induce a sudden boost in performance, a 'honeymoon period'. After listening to an inspirational speaker who is, perhaps, talking from a wheelchair after being paralysed in a fall we may find ourselves thinking 'yes, I suppose that *could* be me' and vow to make a greater effort to cut fewer corners. However, this honeymoon period hardly ever lasts and soon enough we are back to the old levels of performance.

Unless, that is, we *change* something. (In football terms it might be cleverly re-organising the team, better organisation at set pieces or improving fitness levels.) In safety terms we need to change the working environment. Or else the maxim 'if you do what you always did, you get what you always got' soon applies.

BUT IF THEY JUST TOOK MORE CARE!

An average person, fit, rested, and stress free, can only concentrate around 55 minutes an hour. If you're tired, stressed or coming off a split shift it's worse. If you have a workforce of 20,000 that's 16,000 hours a week of away-with-the-fairies zombie time *minimum*.

'Take care at all times' simply can't work. However, if we acknowledge this and get into the good habit of tidying up poor housekeeping when we are bright and alert ... then that trip hazard isn't there when we come back around the corner away with the fairies 10 minutes later.

GOOD HABITS

On training courses I often use some real-life CCTV footage of a young man being knocked off a motorbike by a driver undertaking an illegal U-turn to escape a traffic jam. The motorcyclist is compliant as he wasn't speeding and had every right to be using the outside lane. However, he wasn't driving proactively. (Proactive driving principles are those such as 'always give yourself the time and space to deal with the mistakes of others as well as your own' and 'assume everyone else is a drunken idiot'.)

I once showed this film to some managers when team training with an ex-special services soldier who was waiting to teach them defensive driving techniques. He said something very interesting:

> *You all know me as someone very risk tolerant [we knew him as ex-SAS] if you saw me riding my motorbike in the woods on a weekend you'd be mortified. But this simply wouldn't have happened to me ... because though I'm very risk tolerant I'm also very risk aware and I'd have noticed the curve in the road reducing visibility, I'd have noticed all those frustrated drivers and that there was no barrier separating them from me – and without thinking about it I've have moved to the inside lane to give myself some space.*

As well as a simple demonstration of the American behavioural safety expert Scott Geller's assertion that 'safety must be part of the very DNA of a company' it also illustrates a key point about behavioural safety.

Often when we're tired and distracted the *only* thing that *can* save us are our good habits.

BEHAVIOUR, HEINRICH AND PROCESS SAFETY

It's worth acknowledging that the Heinrich ratios do vary depending on the behaviours in question and the potential outcomes. Some of these behaviours are frequent and reasonably trivial in terms of likelihood (though note that, as above, even trips on flat surfaces cause multiple fatalities every year).

Others are less frequent but more likely to cause fatalities – a steeper triangle if you like. This of course is especially true when we look at process safety issues.

However, the two things aren't separate, but interlink and overlap. A good example of an overlap would be the housekeeping on the Piper Alpha oil platform, which was notoriously poor. (Piper Alpha was the North Sea oil platform that exploded in 1988 with the loss of 167 lives.)

Any meaningful analysis of the poor housekeeping before the accident would have taken the auditor straight to the permit-to-work system. (The permit-to-work system weaknesses are perhaps considered *the* key cause of the explosion.) The permits contained a 'housekeeping put right?' element which, in the light of the poor housekeeping, would have demonstrated clearly a tick-box mentality lacking control. Obviously this would have been a very useful issue to have addressed in early 1988.

Indeed, much unsafe behaviour will be caused in large part by complex organisational weaknesses around communication, ergonomics, staffing and resource that can have devastating organisational consequences.

Therefore, although the dedicated safety conversation that this book covers can never take the place of effective and interlinked systems, monitoring and auditing it certainly should *complement* them and a good conversation really should often seek to directly *address* these in-depth issues when possible. Even when it doesn't directly address them an intelligent open conversation even about something as 'relatively trivial' as housekeeping or PPE compliance could lead to an underlying cause that could be instrumental in causing something catastrophic.

SUMMARY OF KEY POINTS

To reiterate, therefore, safety excellence is about cultural excellence which is in large part about *behavioural* excellence. The next few chapters discuss this notion of safety leadership excellence. Safety leadership is vital to safety excellence per se and before we get to the safety conversation itself let me introduce safety leadership more generally.

(2) Safety Excellence and Leading Safe Practice

In the chapter I will cover:

- Strategic high level safety (briefly).

- Address the principles behind devoting time to a 'walk and talk'.

- Discuss the opportunity a 'walk and talk' gives to genuinely 'lead' the way the inspirational speakers say we should.

- Summarise the output of transformational leadership.

- Summarise two new and hugely influential concepts – one general and one safety specific which help put theory I've covered into context.

- Close with a good old-fashioned checklist of suggested issues to look out for – during a walk and talk or at any time.

STRATEGIC SAFETY

It's said 'you get the safety levels senior management want – all else is just detail and case study'.

One of our clients is considered very much the H&S leader in their field. This stems not from any work we've done with them lately but from an incident at a funeral some 11 years ago when they were very average in terms of safety standards. An employee had been killed and at the funeral a rather apprehensive MD was approached by the widow who instead of attacking or abusing him (as he expected) thanked him sincerely for showing her husband the respect of attending. Relieved and humbled he made himself a promise ...

Obviously this book cannot be of much use where there is little high level commitment to improve. Excellent safety management at a *strategic* level is always essential. Two other examples of that: we have a client that bought into an industry (waste disposal) but found in practice that because of historical contracts the promise 'safely or not at all' simply couldn't be kept if a profit was to be made. They exited. Another client (in the offshore oil and gas industry) has a rule that they will, for any number of commercial reasons, subcontract a high risk activity. But they have a rule that, in order to maximise control, they will only subcontract it *once* ... as they know that each time an activity is contracted a little more control is lost and a little more risk and variability added.

These examples reflect a genuinely high level of commitment to safety excellence. Organisations like this will often benchmark themselves against acknowledged industry leaders. Nothing can replace this but a good walk and talk can help an organisation understand that things are not as good as assumed.

WHERE A 'WALK AND TALK' FITS IN

WE MUST DEVOTE THE TIME TO SHOW LEADERSHIP VISIBLY

First, the 'walk and talk' simply gives a practical demonstration that safety is indeed as important as it's claimed to be in the values statements and visions that a company has. To show '*visible* felt leadership' as it is sometimes known. If you are seen to be devoting time to it, the workforce is more likely to believe you really mean it.

You may of course address related environmental and health issues at the same time as safety. I do feel that less than a half-hour walk a week really isn't enough to achieve this 'visibility'. (Some senior people in the field like the ex DuPont manager Peter McKie recommend at least 30 minutes a day.) Though everything including profit and economic viability interlink and overlap of course a conversation that is primarily 'welfare' focused is key even if it's the planet's welfare.

TO LOOK ACTIVELY FOR THE HOLES IN THE SYSTEM BECAUSE THEY ARE ALWAYS THERE!

Let's assume that your company has broadly reached compliance in its systems and procedures. It has good training, robust induction and risk assessment processes and up-to-date safety management systems. However, like all companies, what it says in the file and what happens in practice are not always the same and the inevitable 'holes in the system' need investigating and plugging. This is particularly so given most companies' constant need to change and update.

The key thing is not to let the problems find us – we must go out and proactively find them! There is a very well known '(fail to) spot a big gorilla amidst mingling basketball players' clip. (As I write this in 2012 it's just about to be retired as a training exercise as nearly everyone has now seen it.) What it illustrated of course is the point that if you walk the site looking *only* for safety issues you'll not see a little more, you'll see 10 times as much than if you look for safety issues whilst going about your day job. (In the exercise the 'day job' is represented by counting passes between fast mingling.)

WE CAN ONLY LEARN WHY OUR PEOPLE DO WHAT THEY DO FROM TALKING TO THEM

The third reason for the walk and talk strand is the Elvis 'walk a mile in a man's shoes' rule crossed with Reason's 'Just Culture' model and Dekker's 'New Model' of Human Error. (If you're unfamiliar with them they are covered in Chapter 4.) Basically, these models show that the value for money we get for our investments in safety improvement is limited by how well we *genuinely* understand why someone has done what they have done.

This can *only* be achieved by talking to them in a way that makes them comfortable enough that they'll be honest with you. Again, I'll be coming back to the practicalities of this issue in the rest of the book.

So far I've tried to make the case that an organisation needs it front line managers proactively on site looking for the inevitable safety issues that are always out there. However, whilst they are out on site looking for issues it's also vital that they take the opportunity to effectively and proactively *lead* safety. The next chapter looks briefly at safety leadership.

HOW A GOOD SAFETY LEADER BEHAVES

Picture an office scene from the UK or US sitcom *The Office*. I'm not talking about the idiotic office manager lead character but instead the 'Gareth' character in the UK version – the slightly strange chap who's the closest thing on the show to a front line supervisor. (If you haven't seen either version he's a pompous, officious, deluded, self-important buffoon. And that's on a good day.) If you have ever watched the programme you'll be well aware of the emotional response of the intelligent and sane 'nice one' who sits opposite and reports to him. Incredulous and despairing at best – utterly appalled at other times …

Can you imagine the reaction if this dubious 'Gareth' character was tasked with leading any sort of safety project or programme? Can I suggest that the likelihood of any sort of success would be zero … because the very *best* response he'd get from his colleagues would be total apathy? It's the real psychology behind this fictional example that is covered by the research I have based this book on.

It's often said that the difference between a leader and a manager is that leaders need followers and that by definition a good leader has *willing* followers. True, I'd argue, and very applicable to safety.

The Australian writer David Broadbent describes three types of leader, which frames this debate very well I think. He suggests these leaders are:

- the fireman;

- the policeman;

- the knight.

The 'fireman' is 'reactive' of course – invisible until something goes wrong. The 'policeman' is primarily about actively seeking out transgressions and ensuring basic compliance. What we need ideally is a workforce full of the third type of leader, proactive 'knights'. Supervisors leading from the front with passion, honour and integrity! This book is an attempt to describe what such a knight looks like and how they behave.

Research shows that the best leaders – the 'knights' if you like – lead in what is known as a 'transformational' way. Moving from the gung-ho Australian call to arms to something a bit more behavioural, the transforming leader:

- leads by example;

- uses (sincere) praise as often as possible;

- coaches (selling) when they can, rather than telling;

- involves the workforce in safety as much as possible.

All the research suggests, unsurprisingly, that high levels of performance are generated in any aspect of work led in this way. (The well-known analogy that explains why is that pulling string is easy ... pushing it next to impossible.) To link to an earlier chapter it's largely through these behaviours that the workforce learn 'what we want, what we really want'. Applied to productivity but not equally to safety then ... you'll have a productive workforce rather than a safe one.

In the simplest terms organisations with world class safety simply apply this approach to both productivity *and* safety.

LEADING BY EXAMPLE

Just one example of a leader not following the safety rules themselves gives a green light to anyone else not to follow them. It is an utter disaster for any safety culture.

We'll talk about this in more detail later under 'Setting the Tone'. For now it's worth stating that (as above) ideally there will be a minimum number of rules and that these will be sensible, fair and easy to follow.

RECOGNITION, PRAISE AND COACHING

Have you have ever watched a 'senior manager working undercover on the shop floor' programme? They always end up saying 'ah, *now* I know what I need to do' don't they? Indeed in the latest version of the UK programme *Undercover Boss* I made a point of counting how many of the bosses claimed to have learnt a huge amount. It was all of them, of course, and it illustrates the point that we best learn about the ins and outs of a job from talking to the person that actually *does* the job.

This may seem so self-evidently obvious that it doesn't need saying. However, it begs the question: why has nearly every workforce I've ever talked to said that 'management don't talk to us enough'?

This 'learning' element is a recurring theme of the book. However, the main point I'd like to make here is that although all the 'undercover boss' employees smiled widely when told they were getting a pay rise a good 50 per cent actually burst into tears of gratitude when told how great they were and how pleased the boss was to have someone so special work for them. This is because genuine recognition reaches us more deeply than reward. It taps into something more primeval and powerful than money.

Another good example of this would be the Ryder Cup golf match between Europe and the USA. Technically it's an exhibition match, but in September 2012 I watched an American golfer who had calmly won *11 million dollars* just the week before the event look close to a heart attack on the final day of the team event, playing for no money at all.

We'll return to address the practical aspects of this theme in Section Two.

WORKFORCE INVOLVEMENT (AND OBJECTIVE ANALYSIS)

It's said that 'a person most owns what they helped create' because of that investment of time and effort. Another saying that resonates with me suggests 'I'll only impose my idea on you if it's four times better than yours as you'll work three times harder on your own idea than you will on mine'.

The old saying is that pushing string is impossible but pulling it is easy. Well this is true unless it's frozen (with fear perhaps?), in which case we can push it where we want it to go – but then can't do much with it when we get there. It's a good analogy and we really do need to proactively work with these truths of personality and not fight against them.

Another vital element of workforce involvement is that they know the day-to-day realities far better then we ever will. It is 'their job' to know of course. I think that perhaps the key element of any good behavioural process is tapping into the knowledge behind the comment we so often hear mumbled in a canteen: 'I could have told them that years ago … if they'd only bothered to ask …'. Reflecting this objective analysis is covered in great detail in Section Two of this book.

Once you've analysed what's wrong with your systems or understood exactly why the workforce aren't behaving as you'd like, it really helps if the solutions come from the workforce themselves.

THE *OUTPUT* OF TRANSFORMATIONAL LEADERSHIP

It's worth listing the consequences of treating people in this 'transformational' way as it illustrates clearly how the *general* culture benefits and why we should take the trouble to do it.

In the United States they talk about 'discretionary behaviour' and it's stated that without it an organisation simply *cannot* develop a strong safety culture as they will never get beyond 'compliant'. (In Chapter 1 we discussed the limitations of compliance.) In the UK we might refer to these as behaviours as 'above the line behaviour' or 'organisational citizenship behaviours' but regardless of the collective name we give them we are talking about behaviours such as:

- Volunteering to be part of a project or process team or to be a safety rep.

- Undertaking non-mandatory safety training or attending non-mandatory meetings.

- Paying any sort of genuine attention or contributing to a discussion during *mandatory* training or meetings.

- Saying something to a colleague who has put themselves at risk.

- Making an effort to model safe behaviours and practices in front of new starts.

- Taking the time to show new starts the ropes.

- Stopping to clear a housekeeping issue.

- Stopping to call a 'time out' because you're not comfortable with a safety issue.

- Reporting a near miss.

- Responding (totally!) honestly to questions during an incident investigation.

And so on.

As we've already stressed several times, few organisations that have all the systems, training and procedures in place to have acquired compliance certificates on their reception walls are anywhere near as *genuinely compliant* on a daily basis as they'd like to be ... so to deliberately blur the edges between compliance and 'discretionary behaviour' we could describe discretionary behaviour as:

- Complying with a safety requirement when not supervised or when working alone.

Because, as we said at the start, often what should be compliance is actually discretionary – especially if it's late or you're working from a van a long way from base.

But regardless of blurred edges I hope that you'd agree this above list is simply the basic behaviours we'd all like to see our workforce undertaking. It's certainly what we want when we get inspirational speakers in, set up behavioural safety processes, or launch 'hearts and minds' initiatives.

THREE FINAL CONCEPTS – NUDGES, GUERRILLA WARFARE AND THE 'MINDFUL' SAFETY CULTURE

This short section attempts to summarise some of the most leading edge thinking that sets the context for this entire book.

- The vital *symbolic* importance of key behaviours and events.

- The importance of always being mindful that safety is an on-going 'guerrilla war'.

- The 'mindful' safety culture.

TOILET BOWLS IN AMSTERDAM – 'NUDGE' THEORY AND HOW QUICKLY WE CAN COMMUNICATE WHAT WE REALLY WANT (FOR GOOD OR BAD!)

If you've already heard of nudge theory you'll know that the most famous example is the well placed painted ceramic fly on the Amsterdam toilet bowl (Figure 2.1) that most of us men can't help but aim at! This apparently reduces splashing by a full 50 per cent, with associated savings in cleaning costs and the environmental impact of cleaning chemicals. (Seriously, imagine trying to match that improvement with a new rule, training or supervision!)

Figure 2.1   The fly in the urinal

Source: © Ruslan Kudrin/Dreamstime.com.

'Nudge' theory is a hugely influential concept at the moment with the UK government and the UK Health & Safety Laboratory have a team dedicated to its application. Examples include: empty police vans parked near potential trouble spots; tax forms asking 'are you sure you haven't forgotten anything?' and motorway signs saying 'don't litter – other people don't', which is a nudge with reference to social norms.

Of course the concept of 'nudging' isn't new. If you've ever used paint to mark a floor or a wall to make clear where something goes – or doesn't go – you're arguably used the nudge concept. Though I may be in danger of trampling over academic definitions, in essence I think of it as *any* small and/or simple thing that can have a big influence on people's behaviour.

The word 'but' in the middle of a sentence is a good example. Have you ever been told 'you're a really nice person and I really like you … but …' and had that sentence end well?! This is because we always put the important part of the message after the 'but'. We all know very well when we have a sentence start that way then contain a 'but' that there's a problem coming. However, it doesn't need to be something we're aware of as it can influence us at a subconscious level. Told 'this job needs doing safely *but* by Friday' both parties may be unaware of how the real message was communicated – but communicated it is.

Three famous mainstream examples of small things having a big impact:

UK magician Derren Brown has a trick where he leaves a full wallet in the middle of a busy pavement but inside a red painted circle – then saunters back to pick it up untouched an hour later. People will not reach across the red line.

In the UK in September 2012 a senior government politician had an argument with a policeman during which he allegedly called the policeman a 'pleb' (it's not a swear word but is a highly derogatory UK term for a person perceived to be of lower social class). Just one word but it generated a huge amount of negative feeling and reaction. His entire political party dropped several points in the opinion polls and his political career seemed over. Recently, however, evidence has come to light that he may not have said this at all and public sympathy has increased dramatically.

Around the same time the transcript of the argument between the Premiership footballers John Terry and Anton Ferdinand contained frequent and aggressive uses of every base sexual insult known to man ... though none of which were considered at all noteworthy or offensive either at the time or later. (Nothing offensive that is except for the word 'black' because of the racial connotations – but that's another matter.)

This introduces us to the concept of the 'critical incident' which tells us that *little* things can mean, and teach us, a *lot*. These aren't necessarily 'nudges' as defined by the textbooks but I'd like to include them as the important point is that they may not look important at a glance but their impact is big. ('Minor behaviours, comments or incidents that punch above their weight and have a big impact' isn't exactly a snappy title is it?)

Nearly all footballers swear at each other like Terry and Ferdinand did – it merely tells us something about the general culture of footballers not about the *individual* men involved. However, the politician simply couldn't have blurted out the word 'pleb' without holding an underlying sense of social superiority. In fact, that it popped out *under stress* makes it even more damning and he will simply *never* recover from it politically.

The jeweller Gerald Ratner saw his company's share value drop to £0.02, and was sacked by his own board, after describing his own jewellery as 'crap'. His customers already knew this of course but this indignity nudged huge numbers of them over a line that made buying anything else from him totally unpalatable. (Incidentally, I shared a conference stage with him once – he was extremely funny about the events that he brought on himself rolling out lines like 'so we ended up owing the banks a total of 1 *billion* pounds … (pause) … which back in those days of course was *a lot* of money!')

CRITICAL INCIDENTS, NUDGES AND SAFETY

Managers who fail to follow their own safety rules throw a big negative nudge as it's often said that the worst level you set as a leader is the highest level you can expect from your reports. Other examples might include starting a meeting by saying 'elf and safety first of course', clearly meaning it is to be got out of the way before the important issues can be addressed.

More positively Shell Scandinavia have stopped asking the question 'why did you choose to shut down?' and started to ask instead 'why did you think it safe to start back up?'. You'll note that the technical information in the reports will be the same, 'this happened and we thought this was the cause … so we thought …' but the shadow it throws is entirely different.

Another classic and oft-repeated experiment shows that if a person observes a pro-social act (like helping an elderly person across the road) then they are significantly more likely to undertake that act the next time they have the chance. Importantly they are highly unlikely to be conscious of the reason for their behaviour. We've already talked about peer influence. Behaviour breeds behaviour – positively as well as negatively.

This book is I hope full of references to 'nudges' – small things which make a big difference. In short, if the commitment to excellence isn't there then the workforce will know. If it is we should actively find ways of communicating that to the workforce.

A good quality 'walk and talk' is the perfect vehicle to nudge colleagues in the right direction.

SAFETY IS NOT AN ACADEMIC EXERCISE IT'S A 'GUERRILLA WAR'

Reason's famous Swiss cheese model (Figure 2.2) shows that the more weaknesses there are in an organisation – from strategy management decisions, through supervision and process safety through to individual actions – the more likely the holes in the slices of Swiss cheese are to line up and an accident occur. This model shows that *with the benefit of hindsight* all accidents could have been prevented and it has directly influenced the various 'target zero' campaigns.

I once gave a talk to a shipbuilder about the cheese model and, after thinking about its strategic implications for a while, they approached me and commented 'we should never have agreed to build this ship this way'. It's perhaps the most influential model in all of safety literature. Recently, however, Reason himself has suggested that the model isn't *always* entirely helpful and his later 'knot in the rubber band'

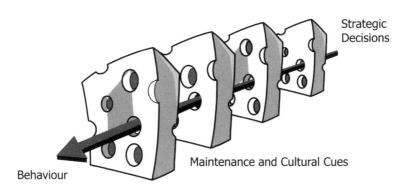

Successive layers of defences, barriers, and safeguards

Figure 2.2   The Swiss cheese model

Source: Adapted from James Reason, 2008.

model illustrates why the target zero campaigns can prove so controversial. (I wish I had a pound for every heated debate about whether target zero is best seen as a concept.)

Before we explore that we need to quickly consider the role of hindsight.

The hindsight model (see Figure 2.3) illustrates that with hindsight the negative outcome that we are investigating looks inevitable as A follows B follows C. However, if we put ourselves in the shoes of the individuals concerned we often see that, *at the time*, several other outcomes looked (and indeed *were*) equally likely. Only *after* the event does the sequence seem inevitable.

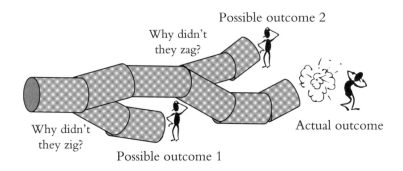

Why didn't
they zag?

Possible outcome 2

Why didn't
they zig?

Possible outcome 1

Actual outcome

Figure 2.3   Hindsight model

Source: © Sidney Dekker, 2006.

THE KNOT IN THE RUBBER BAND MODEL

Imagine a knot in the middle of a large rope and a tug-of-war team on either end (see Figure 2.4). When the left-hand side is winning the company is safe – when the right-hand side is winning then the company is in danger. When the teams are drawing and the knot is in the middle then there is a genuine balance of safety and productivity. (This could be considered a version of the famous 'Balanced Scorecard' concept.)

Reason says that once we start work in the modern world then all sorts of pressures will automatically try and pull the rope away from balance – such as changes in material prices, contractors who don't perform as they promised they would and unexpected delays. It doesn't have to be an infamous 'black swan' that causes problems, a few white swans swimming in harmony will do just fine! (The concept of a 'Black Swan' is being used more and more in articles and the media to describe where something unlikely but devastating actually happens. BP's Deepwater Horizon, the New York storm

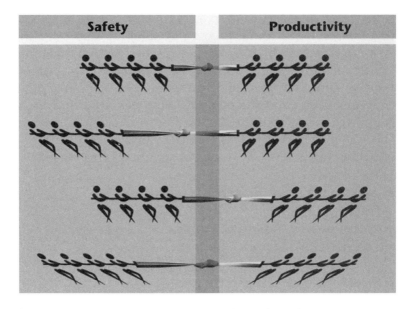

Figure 2.4   The knot in the rubber band
Source: Adapted from Reason, 2008.

and the Japanese Tsunami are famous examples. It is used to encourage in-depth 'what if?' worst case scenario thinking.)

The key is to not ever become overstretched so that the knot moves from a position of genuine balance so that the company is vulnerable. When vulnerable, an incident is more likely of course and investigators will take a dim view when it's seen in hindsight that the organisation had overstretched and were indeed 'an accident waiting to happen'.

Practical application

To return to my shipbuilding example we can say that in an ideal world we wouldn't build ships this way but it is, of course, *not* an ideal world. A more pragmatic view would be to say that *somebody* was bound to agree to build the ship this way so it might as well be us as we need the work. Consequently pockets of vulnerability were *inevitably* going to pop up from time to time and from place to place even if, overall, the culture is strong and the planning thorough. The trick then is to be geared to spot these emerging vulnerabilities quickly and respond promptly. This is entirely analogous to the key principles of UK HSG 48 which covers human error and says:

- Design the job so that error is unlikely.

- Make sure you have mechanisms in place to spot it when it (inevitably) happens.

- Make sure you can respond quickly.

Following on from this Reason suggests safety is best thought of as an on-going *guerrilla war* and like any such war you can't win it in the long run but you can delay defeat almost inevitably. To do this you'll need keen intelligence and data and to use whatever resources you have at your disposal cleverly.

Some managers I've spoken to report that although they buy into the *concept* of target zero the *reality* can seem daunting – even de-motivating. If you have 20,000 workers worldwide then the first lost time injury is likely to arrive early in the new year no matter how excellent your safety standards. What's vital is that you don't become despondent and fatalistic about this reality and the rubber band model seems to be one that managers find best expresses their experience.

This book is of course intended to an extent as a pocket guide on 'how to fight an effective guerrilla safety war'!

THE 'MINDFUL' SAFETY CULTURE

In a similar vein to Reason's rubber band model is the concept of the 'mindful' safety culture. The highly influential Australian writer Andrew Hopkins has studied the causes of major accidents all over the world and insists that organisations must be 'mindful' if they are to have a strong safety culture.

This mindfulness must come from the top and Hopkins says bluntly that 'leaders set the tone and managers have to live with that'. He's being simplistic and provocative, of course, to start a debate (and admits as much) as it's the supervisors who set the tone day to day – though always taking their cue from senior management.

The mindfulness notion is in complete accord with the other most influential writers on the subject whether we are considering James Reason's concept of a 'vulnerable' organisation or Scott Geller's 'Total Safety Culture' where he stresses safety can't be a *priority* ('priorities change daily and are political') it must be a *core value*, embedded in the very DNA of the company so that's it very much 'what we do around here'. In short, it's a version of Aubrey Daniels' assertion that 'we get the safety standards that senior management want – no more, no less'.

Hopkins stresses that good safety leadership will involve losing sleep thinking about 'how do I know XYZ wont happen?'. This is analogous to the core DuPont philosophy that if you're not actively pushing forwards you're almost certainly drifting backwards.

The intention of this book is to use the 80:20 or 'Pareto' principle (where you get 80 per cent of the output from the first 20 per cent of input) to give managers practical tools that will allow any organisation to positively address the key elements of these principles.

SUMMARY OF KEY POINTS

This section has made the case that day-to-day behaviour is vital, whether it is directly determining the risk levels or helping set the tone and therefore triggering others' risky behaviour. It stresses that there is always bad news to be found and that the best companies proactively seek these weaknesses out rather than wait for the weaknesses to find them.

SUGGESTED ISSUES TO DISCUSS

I know that some readers will look at the reference section and order books so that they can read up on some theories outlined above. Others, on the other hand, will be very keen to move onto something more practical. With the later in mind particularly I'd like to end this first half of the book with a suggested list of questions and/or issues that any manager can consider at any time. I'm hoping these will also work as a review of points raised.

One thing I'll absolutely *guarantee*, however. Even if you're working in an organisation with a proactive focus and a genuinely strong safety culture – you won't like *all* the answers!

Ask yourself:

- Do people know who is responsible for each element of the safety process or do 'two people think they are, so no one actually is'.

- Are tool box talks and weekly briefs clear, user-friendly and with understanding confirmed (not just knocked off with a 'sign here' [it's your signature I need and I'm not too bothered if you don't even speak the language in question]).

- Do risk assessments involve genuine reflection and objective thought? Or are they more 'photocopy, sign, file'.

- Is it easy to communicate concerns upwards or does the organisational structure make this difficult if not totally impossible. For example, what do you do if you need to go *through* the person you're concerned about? (And you know for a fact they are *not* going to see this as a learning opportunity!)

- Are the people responsible for writing systems and procedures empowered to ensure they are actually followed?

- Do the people who write the systems and procedures actively consult the end users as a systematic part of the design process?

- Do 'good news audits' produce an automatic sceptical response as lots of infamous incidents were preceded by a string of positive audits – for example Piper Alpha?

(It's worth remembering the Andrew Hopkins quote 'a string of continuous good news? That's not realistic and *really* should set alarm bells ringing!')

- Proactively look at the trends in the reporting system. Are there divisions, shifts or other demographics that hardly ever report? If so, this probably isn't good news – dig into it and find out what the blockages are and why.

- Conversely, has someone raised a safety issue that was basically ignored? (A characteristic of nearly all major incidents.)

- Consider how senior management respond to *bad* news. A response as simple as simply *looking* inconvenienced is problematic ... (I once asked an MD at a board meeting if he ever responded negatively to a safety issue being raised and he was adamant 'never!' I asked 'not even with the eyes?' and the whole room burst into laughter as he was notorious for this. Luckily he wasn't a defensive man – he laughed at himself and we were off ...).

- Follow an incident that is mentioned in conversation through the reporting system. How far did it get? What was learned? What was the done with this learning? Even the best companies with highly expensive tracking systems will find that the answers to these questions are concerning.

- When looking at the analysis that flows from incidents imagine you have a big red 'why?' stamp. Do any points noted beg asking this question – if so the investigation probably hasn't gone deep enough and you're targeting a symptom not a root cause.

- Ask has there been any cost-cutting recently – or perhaps a 'renegotiated' contract? If so was it risk assessed really thoroughly for the 'law of unintended consequences' or were assumptions made that all will be well? With that law in mind it's always worth checking who is being rewarded for what. Some examples:

  - Consider where the *number* of 'walk and talks' is monitored but not the *quality*. Where this is the case you'll often find that, in order to meet targets, a flurry of poor quality ones are undertaken at the end of the month.

  - Procurement are rewarded for cutting costs but no one checks if any false economies result as a consequence (e.g. cheaper PPE that no one actually wears because it's uncomfortable or isn't fit for purpose; cheap components that fail and leak; manpower cuts that mean there is genuinely not enough time to thoroughly think, plan and check).

  - Bonuses that are paid only on lost time incidents so management focus on these and not on *process* safety issues (as at Texas City where the findings of the wide ranging Baker report into the explosion at the BP plant in 2005 could be summarised as 'they put so much effort into making sure no one tripped over, then using these figures as *proof* of excellent safety standards even in the face of maintenance cuts they let the place blow up').

And last but most certainly not least:

- The way many contractors are remunerated and selected – because as you well know the term 'a whole can of worms' was probably coined with subcontractors in mind. The old saying 'cheap, quick, good quality – please pick any two from the three' summarising the issue perfectly.

CONCLUSION

The list above is not exhaustive of course but it should give anyone plenty to be mindful about! You can see that its primary aim is to imbue a sceptical, proactive and thoughtful mindset that is far in advance of a manager who's merely been trained in the legislation of compliance. It's the mindset of a streetwise guerrilla fighter if you like Reason's analogy.

Some training may well be required so that your front line supervisors understand the *why* behind the mindset as well as the *what.* However, with Scott Geller's memorable training v. education example in mind we still need a mechanism to genuinely embed this mindset. (Geller stresses that good *training* is much more in-depth and hands on than basic education. To illustrate the point he asks how we'd feel if our teenage children came home from school announcing that next week they will be doing sex education. Then the week after that they were moving on to some *training* ...)

Aristotle observed that humour is merely common sense speeded up. We laugh because instantly we know exactly what Geller means here. The question for the reader is how often have you seen a session that really should have been a *training* session for a limited number of workers that was instead a short briefing session for many more?

Ideally, introduced with some suitable training, we need to roll-out a robust, user-friendly and simple 'walk and talk' approach that is based on objective analysis, open and honest communication and which allows the whole workforce a regular opportunity to contribute to the safety culture. Section Two outlines a simple five-step model that aims to achieve this.

Safety Contacts

The safety contact involves five simple but distinct phases. To be more specific it needs an appropriate combination of the following five phases:

1. Introduce Yourself, Break the Ice and Set the Tone.

2. Analysis.

3. Coaching.

4. Eliciting a Promise(?)

5. Closing Out.

One of the aims of this book is to provide the reader with some tools to help them decide what 'appropriate' means in each individual situation.

WALK AND TALK AND WORKFORCE 'BEHAVIOURAL SAFETY'

This book isn't about behavioural safety, but just for the record, the overlap with that theme is primarily with the second step – *analysis*. Ideally, a company will, in time, introduce a behavioural programme that involves the workforce directly in the analysis of unsafe behaviour. An excellent way of doing this is through limited time duration *project* teams who are trained in behavioural analysis techniques and who are allowed to choose issues they want to address. Any 'high impact: low cost' solutions they come back with should be implemented as soon as possible and as much mileage as possible made of them in in-house magazines and other internal communication channels.

Alternatively, some form of *on-going* peer-to-peer observation process might be also adopted and if an observation process is used then the behavioural measurement from this might be used to provide data for feedback charts. This is what is often referred to as 'full' behavioural safety, has its roots in the quality work of Demming and has much in common with Six Sigma methodologies. To give you a flavour of what I mean imagine the following workforce-run canteen meeting:

> *As you know, the volunteer committee decided to look at PPE initially and the collated score from the unannounced measures we've been taking over the last month is 66%, as can be seen on the big colourful chart on the wall here. Now, in the first week people hurriedly put their PPE on as we approached, but once you all realised scores were just an anonymous tick in the box you all settled down and we've discounted that first week and feel these scores are accurate – based on a suitably sized and randomised sample as they are. We'll update that chart on a weekly basis and add categories such as Housekeeping, Use of Tools, Plant/ Personnel Interaction and Access to Heights as we go. Now, the question is what can we realistically get up to by the end of next month and most importantly what are the obstacles to getting there?*

There's also a behavioural safety overlap with the *coaching* element of the walk and talk too, where you'll see that key components of that section – being listened to and being actively involved in decision making – are totally analogous with any good behavioural safety process.

Indeed a 'walk and talk' based on analysis and coaching will be 100 times as effective in reducing unsafe behaviour in the medium to long term as a 'if you can walk on hot coals you can do anything ... so go back to the shop floor and be safe' initiatives.

Behavioural safety is anything that addresses behaviour. Good behavioural safety is anything that improves it in a sustainable manner. An inspirational speaker or emotional DVD is an excellent way to raise awareness and motivation. But neither is sustainable.

SUGGESTED FREQUENCY OF SAFETY CONTACTS

Aubrey Daniels in *Safe by Accident?* stresses that there are three levels of learning. There's basic learning, then mastery of the basics, and then, finally, *fluency*. Basic learning involves someone knowing how to do a task and being able to do it without fault with a lot of concentration. 'Mastery' can be described as 'I can now do it with a degree of confidence' and tends to be achieved after 30 or so practices. For example, imagine learning to play golf or work as a volunteer on the Samaritans' helpline – or any other skill of that type. At what stage would you stop saying 'I'm learning to' and start saying 'I am a ...'.

Fluency, however, describes the stage when these skills are embedded to a similar extent to your driving skills over time. I like to think I'm a reasonably fluent speaker at conferences these days – but it took a few years and I'm certainly better now than I was once I'd done my 30 and had become broadly competent ...

This notion of *fluency* is addressed by another US safety writer, Scott Geller, who says that safety must be something truly embedded as part of the very DNA of a company. (As in 'our culture is what we do around here ... *automatically*'.) Indeed, Geller was one of the first to say 'Stop saying safety is the No1 priority, priorities change and priorities are political! It needs to be embedded as a core *value*' (because if there *is* a number one priority it's making enough profit or generating enough turnover to stay in business. Or if it's an animal charity it's raising funds and rescuing animals, etc.).

A genuinely embedded core value was well illustrated by the 'around the world' sailor Pete Goss when he turned back to rescue a fellow competitor in the Arctic. His inspirational talk builds to a simple question from the audience, which is 'how long did it take you to abandon the month long race and turn back when you realised it had to be you?' His answer 'oh 4 or 5 seconds ... it's the values of the sea ... I didn't even need to think about it'. (His challenge is 'can you match that with your safety statements?' and from the uneasy shuffling in the audience it was clear not many felt they could.)

A good example of embedded behaviour might be the yard manager of a mine who reminded me to reverse park when I once forgot to. He did it firmly but in a naturally comfortable and friendly way that told me he'd done it many times before. And as I looked around I was very embarrassed to note I was the only person not to have reverse parked!

Which all leads up to me making a simple point: what do you imagine we think when companies tell us they have management's commitment to undertake at least one or two safety contacts a year!? Even doing one a month means it will take you around three years to reach basic mastery. So I'd like to suggest that one a month is an absolute *minimum*.

This is important for another reason too. If our trainee supervisors and managers do not go out and use the behaviours we've requested how can we give them feedback and embed the behaviours?

EMBEDDING TRAINING

WHO AND WHAT

A basic motivation theory developed by Victor Vroom explains why so many training courses are a waste of money (Figure S2.1). To be effective, training first needs to explain *what* we want people to do and be clear *who* needs to do it. (The expression 'if two people think they're responsible then no one is' applies.)

WHY

However, we also need to take the trouble to explain *why* – or the average worker will feel slighted and be apt to drag their heels. No one likes to be told 'because I say so' even when they are only 10 years old. More than this, without an appreciation of the reasoning behind a requested behaviour or action we aren't best placed to adjust when something unexpected happens.

HOW

We then need to address *'how'* to do what we want them to do, because if an employee is worried that they can't do something competently they'll find any excuse not to do it at all in case they make a fool of themselves.

VALUED OUTCOME – WHAT'S IN IT FOR ME?

Finally, we need to consider whether the individual sees any *value* in the outcome sought – whether that is analysis, praising, coaching or challenging. Importantly we need to think of this combination of *'what and why'*, *'how'* and *'perceived as valued'* as not something we stack on top of each other but rather as something we multiply – so a low score *anywhere* means a low score overall and motivation will be poor.

Vroom

Why
for example:
– Heinrich
– Just Culture

Basic/generic skills
for example:
– Assertion
– Ice Breaking
– Presentation Skills

 X X

What
for example:
– Analysis
– Communication

More advanced /specific skills
for example:
– Five Whys Analysis
– Coaching

Embedding the new behaviour
for example:
– Day to Day Feedback
– Formal Appraisal Items

Figure S2.1   Vroom/Marsh model

It's vital that the typical front line supervisor be taught to value the outcome of these behaviours by the organisation. An experienced safety professional of my acquaintance summarises it thus:

> *If the behaviours requested are not considered career enhancing in the smoke shack six months after the training course then they won't be happening and you'll have wasted your money.*

We achieve this through *formal* and *informal* feedback. Formal feedback involves giving safety items prominence in the appraisal – some companies don't include safety in the formal appraisal at all or give them only perfunctory coverage on the day. (By which I mean both the appraiser and the person being appraised clearly relax a little through these items whilst collecting their thoughts before getting back to something more important! As an experiment try videoing a session and playing it back with the sound off, rating the participants' animation!)

Informal feedback can be summarised with our adaptation of Aubrey Daniels' 'tick' rating. He suggests when we see a worker acting safely – a tick! However, should we see a supervisor praising a worker for acting safely (as requested on a recent leadership course perhaps) two ticks! A manager taking the time to praise a supervisor he's seen praising a worker acting safely … three ticks! I'm sure you get the idea and it's in *this* way the behaviours we want more of are *embedded* as 'the way we do things around here'. It's not from the training course appraisal scores no matter how good they are.

The reverse would be a manager seeing a supervisor fail to challenge an unsafe act (as requested on a recent course) and saying nothing. No ticks for anyone. And no embedded behaviour change at all likely either.

FOLLOW UP

A useful technique is to produce a simple set of scales addressing the key behaviours requested during a training course. Then ask some of the workers to rate them. For example:

How do you rate your supervisor's praise and feedback?

5   Often praises routine safe behaviour

4

3   Rarely praises safe behaviour/praises only exceptional behaviour

2

1   Never praises safe behaviour

(A suggested basic six-item checklist is included in Appendix 2.)

These scores can be collated with the scores of other items addressing such issues as challenging, coaching, leading by example, involving the workforce and analysis. Then the overall score can be *multiplied* by the fabulous happy sheet scores from the 'what, why and how' training session to give us an overall score of training efficacy.

Done thoroughly, an organisation will too often find itself pondering an extremely disappointing *overall* total score. In addition, it will be highly likely that safety climate surveys will be showing little improvement, anecdotal evidence will be suggesting 'things don't feel all that different' and accident rates will be inching rather than leaping forward.

I would like to make the assertion that in my experience in the medium to long term *at least 80 per cent* of the efficacy of a training course is in the follow up and embedding ... (any hard research data very much welcome. Any interested students please do get in touch).

In short we need to:

- Train our managers and supervisors in *what* to do and who's to do it.

- Explain *why* they need to do it.

- Give them the *skills* and tools to ensure they can do them well.

- Ensure they do them *often* enough to master the basics.

And:

- Give them systemic feedback to ensure they refine and *embed* these behaviours.

BEFORE HIS INTERPERSONAL SKILLS TRAINING, PAUL'S ATTEMPTS AT CHALLENGING UNSAFE BEHAVIOUR DIDN'T ALWAYS WORK OUT

③ Introduce Yourself and Set the Tone

In this section I will discuss:

- Ice-breaking.

- Setting the tone.

- Building trust.

- Leading by example.

FIRST SOMETHING HUGELY IMPORTANT – MODELLING (OR 'DON'T BE THE T*T WITH THE TOUPE')

A key thing you *must always do* yourself is to model safety at all times (whether undertaking a safety conversation or not). It's often said that the highest standard you can expect from those that work for you is the lowest standard you set yourself. All managers and supervisors are role models whether they like it or not (so are safety representatives, experienced workers and the charismatic individuals who are admired in the canteen).

One of our clients had the former UK Prime Minister Gordon Brown visit a site (Figure 3.1) and decline to wear eye protection during a site visit. Management let him get away with it because of the inconvenience of refusing to walk him about, but wish they hadn't. The CEO still says 'I've paid for that decision every day since. The lads didn't say, as we hoped, "I'd have done the same if I'd been in Vick's shoes" … they leapt on it with glee and every tool box talk and briefing and *especially* at any disciplinary we get "what about Gordon Brown!". If I could turn the clock back I would!'

Figure 3.1   Gordon Brown visits Govan
Source: © Istockphoto/Edstock.

I've since had an experience that you might find amusing.

One of our clients had a visit from a senior chap from HQ who flatly refused to don his hard hat during a site visit. The local secretaries quickly spoke to their contacts at HQ and found out that it was because he wore a wig and was worried it would come off and embarrass him. As well as causing our PPE enhancement process no end of problems for months you might be amused to know that even before he'd even left the site he was widely know as the 'tit with the toupe'. (That's a cleaned up version – the actually alliteration was on the letter 'w' – as in wig.)

It is fair to say then that as well as everything else that went wrong that day the 'maintaining his dignity' plan didn't work quite the way he'd intended!

The first golden rule then is always to follow the rules yourself. (If you find doing so inconvenient then that's really useful because so will a lot of other people and that's a problem that needs proactively addressing. It's covered in depth in the next section.)

SETTING THE TONE

I tried to give an example of setting the tone in the Preface with the two humorous anecdotes. Whilst we're certainly not advocating you start your talk with jokes and funny stories we *are* advocating that you don't plough straight in to the analytical elements.

Instead, take the time to chat to the person a little, starting with a brief introduction of who you are and what you're doing. You might ask:

- How are you?

- What's it like doing your job nowadays?

- What are the safety implications (you might want to refer to any risk assessment)?

Talk about the weekend's sporting events. Just get them talking and at their ease. Time invested in doing this will pay dividends later when you get to the meat of the conversation.

Don't forget that their initial thought will be a concern that you are trying to catch them out ... so they will most likely be wary of you initially. It's said a good political interviewer asks themselves 'why is this lying git lying to me today' and initially we can assume most workers will be asking themselves 'why is this nosey git prying into my business?'

Applying the 'One Minute Manager' golden rule of 'catch a person doing something right' is a useful technique to overcome suspicion. However, be sure to do it naturally by picking something that clearly deserves praise not something that will look trotted out by numbers. For example, 'I'm impressed with the housekeeping ... you look very organised' (if they do) as you walk up is one thing. Looking tongue-tied and, after an uncomfortable silence, blurting out 'er ... you're very tall aren't you!?' quite another.

They are also highly likely to want to be rid of you as fast as possible. This is understandable as no one wants to be interrupted. However one of the few things we like more than we dislike being interrupted is being asked what we *think* and what we *feel*. You'll have been stopped by a market research person I'm sure and tried to get away but if they can stop you and get you talking then often you'll be saying 'and write this down too!' long after their eyes have glazed over and they've got what they needed (... or perhaps that's just me!).

BUILDING TRUST

Studies show that admitting you don't know everything and asking questions increases a person's level of trust in you rather then reducing their respect. Since enhancing trust is something we are all aiming for within companies, asking questions and listening to the answers is a key component of a good safety talk.

Perhaps the best known culture model is that of the 'Bradley Curve'. This model suggests that we need to move from dependent ('I'll act safely but only if you're watching') through 'independent' ('I'll act safely even on my own') to, finally, 'interdependent' where we are each our 'brother's keeper'. Interdependence is about trust and team work and all those 'above the line behaviours' we discussed above under the section on the outcome of genuinely transformational leadership.

As you can imagine trust is a hugely important element of this most advanced element – interdependence – and a good walk and talk most certainly helps build trust.

SOME DOS AND DON'TS

The first *don't* is that whilst a safety conversation may never be entirely convenient it's best not to stop someone when it's extremely inconvenient or even dangerous!

So *do* remember to consider whether talking to them now will be a *little* bit inconvenient or *very* inconvenient!

Do make sure that you *listen* even if you know the answers already. It's getting them comfortable talking to you that's key here.

Avoid asking closed questions if you can – you'll often get closed answers in response. (Closed questions can be answered with a simple 'yes' or 'no' – open questions ask, for example, 'what do you think?') Most people will of course say 'yes' or 'no' if they can, whether or not that's true, just to get rid of you as quickly as possible.

Stay professional and *avoid* becoming too 'matey'. Never step beyond friendly and human and into unprofessional. It might make the session pass nicely for you but you won't have the impact you want by being 'one of the guys'.

SUMMARY OF KEY POINTS

● *Always* lead by example.

● Remember that whilst there will never be an ideal time and location, some times and locations are better than others!

- Be friendly but not overly 'matey'.

- Remember that admitting you don't know everything makes you more trusted.

- Use open questions.

AT REDCAR STEELWORKS, NEW MANAGER BILLY BOB FROM TEXAS FAILS TO ADJUST HIS FEEDBACK STYLE TO LOCAL CULTURE

(4) Analysis

In this chapter I will discuss:

- Human error.

- Just Culture.

- Curious whys and 'five whys'.

- ABC analysis.

- The 'anything inconvenient?' technique.

ANALYSIS

The second stage of the conversation is the analysis of any issues seen or raised. This is where the principles of 'Just Culture' come into play (see Figures 4.1, 4.2 and 4.3). Issues might include failure to wear PPE, poor housekeeping, driving a forklift truck unsafely, or perhaps a tool box talk or brief that lacked impact.

Human Failure

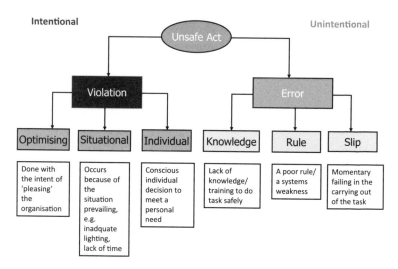

Figure 4.1   Just Culture model

Source: Adapted from Sidney Dekker, 2012.

'Just Culture' is a model that takes the overly simplistic 'no name, no blame' approach forward by stressing that if we analyse objectively we'll find that the majority of unsafe acts happen for a reason that makes, at least, a certain sense if you genuinely understand the root cause.

James Reason (who coined the term and did much of his work in aviation) gives a simple example asking us to consider a worker checking rivets on a plane. He says if the worker has the time, the torch and the gantry, does the job conscientiously but misses as few rivets, this is out-and-out human error. Go away and invent a machine that works better than the human eye. If a worker is working conscientiously but is missing a torch, a gantry or is under time pressure then

Just Culture/HSG 48

FIX

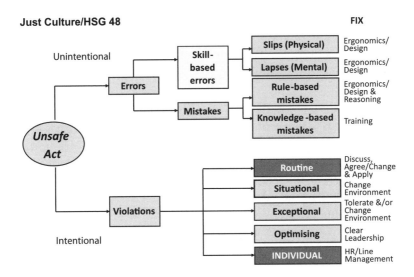

Figure 4.2   Adaptation of the Just Culture model to incorporate HSG/48

Notes: The model above shows the original Just Culture model adapted to incorporate HSG 48 as many companies prefer. Please note that the addition of an 'Exceptional' violation reflects those times when it is adaptive to break the rule. (For example, jumping in the sea from Piper Alpha which was against training but which saved many lives.) All simple models have weaknesses but I think the major weakness of this version is to include 'Routine' as part of the list of violations. For me violations that have become routine nearly always commence life as situational ('I had to get the job done') and/or optimising ('I thought that's what you really wanted'). Only when all error and violation options have been investigated and dismissed can we tick the 'individual' box.

they are blameless and it's an organisational resource issue. Finally consider the worker who has the time, the torch and the gantry but chooses to work quickly from the ground so they can get back to the canteen and their crossword. This is their fault and they should suffer accordingly.

Only in the minority of cases will a person be off on a folly of their own. The key thing here is to be as analytical and learning focused as possible as whatever happens next will be limited by the accuracy of your analysis.

The following is worth stating really bluntly. If you have £100 to spend on safety and 80 per cent of the causes of unsafe acts are physical or cultural and only 20 per cent are individual then you need to spend £80 on changing the physical and cultural issues and only £20 on the people themselves to most effectively use that £100. In my experience many companies get this the wrong way around and 80 per cent is spent on retraining, inspirational speakers, and the like.

Indeed, Sidney Dekker in his hugely influential *Field Guide to Understanding Human Error* would argue that my 80 per cent is actually an underestimate and he (also) says bluntly:

> *human error is not the cause but the effect. Whatever the label (loss of situational awareness, inadequate resources, (even) complacency) human error can never be the conclusion of your investigation. It is the starting point.*

That's worth restating: the efficiency of your response and any use of organisational resources has an upper limit set by the accuracy of your analysis. A couple of quotes from all-time greats:

> *A problem is that if you solved a problem effectively yesterday with a hammer then tomorrow everything is going to look like a nail. (James Reason)*

> *Always walk for a mile in a man's shoes before you judge them. (Elvis)*

JUST CULTURE

If you follow such influential theories as Reason's 'Cheese' and Dekker's 'Just Culture' models you'll find if you analyse objectively that many unsafe behaviours are out-and-out *unintentional* errors caused by design, task demands, ergonomics or lack of training ('I don't know what I'm doing and/or I'm physically or mentally incapable of doing it – especially if I'm tired!').

Further, many conscious *violations* (a deliberate breaking of the rules) are often caused by a workers need to get finished before midnight and encouraged with 'blind eye' syndrome from those around them! (If this weren't the case then 'work to rule' wouldn't be such an effective strategy.) It is true that often an unsafe act is undertaken because the person feels that behaviour was what the company wanted. For example, imagine you do a job well one week and cut a few corners. The only feedback given is 'good job, well done' although management know perfectly well that corners have been cut – or perhaps assume but 'don't ask' so they 'don't formally know'. You guarantee the same corners will be cut again next week. If you wanted to be emotive about it you could almost call this 'grooming'.

In the first section we detailed what a 'mindful' organisation looks like. In doing so we covered dozens of day-to-day events that cue the workforce to a view of what management 'really, really want' that is a long way from world class. Other examples of 'productivity before safety' cues would include having safety as the first item on an agenda (as required) but addressing it in a way that makes it clear we are to get through it as fast as possible so that we can crack on with the *important* stuff.

The core of a 'Just Culture' then is to step back and apply some objective analysis before rushing to judgement. Just asking 'why?' in a genuinely *'curious'* manner will pretty much do it. If you do you'll find that in 80 to 90 per cent of cases you'll learn something interesting even if it's just that there's a systemic *temptation* to cut a corner.

Adopting a 'Just Culture' approach simply can't be done well without talking with and listening to the workforce. It has an additional benefit too. Research shows clearly that the more 'just' the culture is perceived to be, the more effective the *basic* reactive incident reporting and analysis system (let alone anything more proactive) because it maximises objectivity in analysis and more openness in reporting. It also impacts well on spurious claims, turnover, absenteeism, 'presenteeism' and motivation.

I'd like to strongly suggest therefore that talking about transformational safety leadership without explicit reference to Just Culture and 'Why?' analysis is, to me really missing a trick. The legendary Irish rugby player Willie John McBride who captained the British Lions to an unbeaten tour of South Africa in 1974 is certainly one of the most inspirational rugby captains ever. However, though his role was vital, an objective analysis of events would acknowledge that the groundbreaking coaching and preparation the squad received were most probably far more important. An awful lot of thought, analysis and preparation preceded anyone lacing a pair of boots, pulling on the famous jersey and psyching themselves up in the changing room before the match.

On the other hand, although it's *analysis* that gives any human factor process its real 'kick' it must be said that without the 'transformational' leadership behaviours discussed in Section One of this book you could argue that a genuinely learning focused and proactive culture can't get going at all. The two are interlinked and self-supporting.

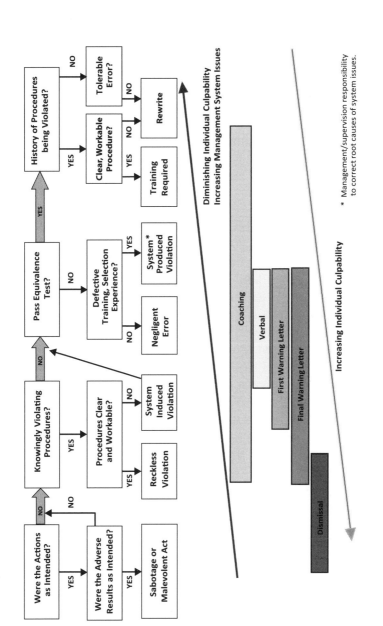

Figure 4.3   Just Culture example

When a workforce are asked to describe the traits of the best safety leader they have seen – one they would trust to keep their children safe – they always include 'trustworthy, consistent, transparent and fair'. Taking the basic analytical model above (Figure 4.3) and validating it with the workforce before systematically rolling it out through human resources is a very good way of helping increase these traits in front line management.

ANALYTICAL METHODOLOGIES: THE 'CURIOUS WHY?'

If a company can double the number of times managers ask the question 'why?' with *curiousity* – and, of course, do something with the answers – then the safety culture will be transformed. I guarantee it. Importantly, it's very much worth stressing that the 'why?' question *must* be asked with a *curious* tone. Ask it aggressively and the person you are talking to will very likely get defensive and clam up.

Even if the answer to this question shows that it *is* the person who is at fault you still learn something. If this is the case that the person you're talking to is indeed 'bang to rights' then a more *robust* response is appropriate. That would be the justice in 'Just Culture' perhaps! It's not easy when you really analyse in depth, however, to come up with a good example of someone who is genuinely 'guilty'.

However, here are four examples I've come across:

- (As above) a worker checks rivets quickly from the ground so they can get back to the canteen and finish their crossword.

- We find a group of workers indulging in a game of darts inside a factory with air powered nail guns. (Or perhaps in an organised forklift truck grand prix.)

- We find a worker walking around a factory with a hole poked in their face mask so they can have a cigarette from time to time.

- A worker has their mandatory safety glasses on but has poked the glass out.

Pretty clear-cut? Not in any of the cases actually ... applying the Elvis rule of walking a mile in their shoes before we judge them, we find that:

The rivet checker: this worker had been doing this job without break or rotation for more than a year. She was bored senseless and had never been certain exactly what she was looking for as her initial training was inadequate ... and when she first started nipping off early her supervisor saw her and said nothing. (Indeed it would have been a bit hypocritical as he did the same when he stood in.)

The darts players and racers: for years considered a perk of doing a 'real man's job' and nearly every manager and supervisor in the place had been involved in these games when they were younger and less senior. Indeed the new owner's mortification at coming across this tradition was met with genuine incredulity by the workers.

The smoker: never pulled up on it before despite being seen hundreds of times over the years by managers who'd done it themselves as foremen when the worker had joined the company.

Missing lenses: this worker was genuinely convinced by the rumour that the plastic lenses would damage his eyesight.

The good news is that by being systematically analytical first any 'justice' is both less frequent and transparently fairer when it is required. This in itself helps move the whole company culture forward.

As intimated, the trick is to then *do* something with all this learning ... which many organisations find very difficult.

At the IOSH rail conference 2011 East Midland trains produced some graphs showing impressive improvements in incident rates and made the comment:

> *for us the key was to stop treating SPADs (signals passed at danger) as events in themselves but as symptoms of a more underlying issue. That shift in mindset was vital.*

A PROACTIVE METHODOLOGY

THE HYPOTHETICAL 'ANYTHING SLOW OR UNCOMFORTABLE?' QUESTION

If no issues have been raised by the initial observation then the person running the safety contact needs to start a hypothetical discussion. There will always be something to be discussed and the question 'anything slow or uncomfortable about doing this job or task safely?' will nearly *always* raise some issues.

The good news is that it's even easier to transform a safety culture by doubling the number of times a manager asks the hypothetical question because in most companies it's simply not being asked *at all*.

THE POWER OF TEMPTATION

Oscar Wilde quipped that he could resist everything 'except temptation'. The UK comedian Stephen Fry explains that he 'always gives in to temptation straight away – it saves time'. We find these quips amusing because we recognise the psychology behind them and this psychology most directly answers the question we are most frequently asked as psychologists: 'why do people do the risky things they do?'

SOME EXAMPLES OF THE POWER OF TEMPTATION

Almost half the UK's MPs had to pay back expenses, having given in to the temptation of over-claiming expenses. (Interestingly, many new MPs who resisted initially gave testimony they came under pressure from the old hands not to 'make them look bad', a classic example of the pervasiveness of existing culture.)

It's also said that the financial crisis of 2008 was triggered by the abundance of cheap credit available in the years leading up to it. To quote Michael Lewis in *The Sunday Times*:

> *The tidal wave of cheap money that rolled across the planet between 2002 and 2007 wasn't just money it was temptation. It offered entire societies the chance to reveal aspects of themselves they could normally not afford to indulge. Entire countries were told 'the lights are out you can do what you want in the dark …' Americans wanted to own homes larger than they*

> *could afford, Icelanders wanted to stop fishing and become investment bankers and the Greeks wanted to be treated as a properly functioning northern European economy but whilst carrying on as normal with an inefficient and corrupt culture but one that was now in the Eurozone and with access to cheap loans.*

It's fair to say that in today's celebrity obsessed culture all famous footballers can sleep around pretty much as they wish – even the ones that look more like Shrek than David Beckham. Given the large number who do give in to this temptation – and find themselves in serious trouble doing so – I suspect that the percentage that give into temptation and get away with it is very high.

What these mainstream examples show is that it is true that we find temptation difficult to resist and the implications for safety are enormous. We really need to talk about ABC analysis.

ABC ANALYSIS

ABC analysis shows us that even where the long-term consequences of behaviour can be very important it's the short-term consequences that mostly determine whether someone behaves in this way. ABC stands for *antecedents, behaviours and consequences. Antecedents* meaning all triggers such as training and signage and anything contextual that's relevant – such as the fact that the person is tired, badly equipped or badly trained.

So, for example, we smoke and drink and eat rich food and skip the gym and hope for the best regarding illnesses such as heart disease and cancer and we speed in our cars to save time even though we know driving is by far the most dangerous thing we'll ever do.

This principle is important at work as when the safe way is slow, uncomfortable or inconvenient we are tempted to cut the corner and 'crack on'. And, of course, we nearly always get away with it which is rewarding and validates our instinctive 'dynamic risk assessment'. However, as explained in Section One the laws of Heinrich's Triangle tell us that one of the corner-cutters will inevitably get hurt sooner or later.

Therefore, I'd argue that where there is a temptation to cut a corner because the safe way is slow or inconvenient in some way this temptation is as systemic a risk as an unguarded drop or unguarded piece of machinery. Because people are people and not robots, unsafe behaviour in these circumstances reflects human nature and it's just a question of how soon someone gets hurt.

We can therefore wait until an incident and find out about these temptations from a (good) accident investigation. Then we can exhort our workers not to give in to such temptations (a thankless task). Or we can proactively get out and about and discover these temptations and, whenever practicable, *design them out* of the workplace.

USING THE INFORMATION

As with a 'why' analysis, any suggestion for improvements that is agreed to be 'high impact: low cost' should be invested in as soon as possible. In addition, the people who came up with the analysis should be lavished with praise both personally and through in-house media such as newsletters.

(We will talk more about the importance of praise in Chapter 5 on coaching.) In addition the organisation should share this best practice as widely as it can.

We are very good at spotting mistakes – it's hot wired into us as people – but we are less good at spotting safe behaviour. Consider the contents of *any* newspaper or TV news programme and how you'd feel if someone asked to 'talk to you about your behaviour'. Blame comes naturally to us – for example how much of your last 'good old gossip' was positive? We need to develop techniques that embed praise as a habit.

Even more motivating than praise is the simple act of listening to someone and then acting on anything sensible they say. We all enjoy warm words but actually *applying* someone's knowledge and experience is as sincere as praise can get – with the individual certain to feel valued and useful.

SUMMARY OF KEY POINTS

Finally, as a reminder of the points above here's a checklist of questions to ask the workforce, the answers to which might help you understand what's really going on:

- Why did you do that? ('Why' asked *curiously*.)

- Is there anything slow, uncomfortable or inconvenient about doing this job safely?

- To distinguish an *error* from a *violation* the question is '*can* they do it safely if their lives depended on it?' If they can't then it's an error and we need to talk to the training department and/or an ergonomist.

- To distinguish an *'optimising/situational'* violation from an *'individual'* violation the question is *'realistically,* can they do it safely without meaningful inconvenience or discomfort?' Again, if they *can't* then we need a design solution – unless the discomfort would be entirely social (because it's not custom and practice and they'd stand out from their colleagues). In this case we need to look at the *culture* ...

Other questions worth asking yourself (or the person being talked to if they trust you enough to answer):

- How often does this unsafe act occur?

- How many do it?

- Has it ever been seen by a supervisor and, if so, what did they do when they saw it?

- What did they do when they saw it done safely?

- What do peers say if they see it?

TRAINING FOLLOW UP TO EMBED SAFE WORKING

The learning opportunities that flow from these question lists are self-evident. Training supervisors *how* to ask them and *why* isn't difficult. However, I do stress that that's only 20 per cent of the culture change. The organisation really must, some months later, invest some time asking the workforce how often these questions have been asked of them – and how skillfully – to derive the other 80 per cent benefit.

(5) Coaching

In this chapter I will discuss:

- Basic coaching – the 'feedback fish'.

- Ownership and involvement.

- Reward and praise.

- Listening.

- Rational data and illustration.

- Assertion – always middle bubble please!

The coaching element of the safety contact is all about the 'inspirational' leadership behaviours we discussed at the start of the book. Certainly it's often said that the worst way to get a person to do something is to tell them to do it. This seems true of the typical western worker; we are a contrary and complicated lot are we not?

Developing a good style is important to coaching as if you are threatening or annoying they'll not want to work with you and when you want to consider 'what if?' scenarios, they'll be thinking 'who the hell are you ...?' Therefore, you need to introduce yourself, break the ice, put them at ease and avoid confrontation.

Sometimes the person you are talking to may be provocative or incorrect but you should avoid taking them on and/or 'putting them right' whenever possible. (Unless of course that's unavoidable or appropriate – after all, although we're advocating that a good guerrilla fighter is first and foremost clever and thoughtful, they do need to strike decisively at times.) Use techniques like the 'flat bat' neutral paraphrase to confirm you're listening even if you don't necessarily agree. For example, 'so what you're saying is that all management are paper-pushing Muppets who haven't done a proper day's work in their lives and therefore know nothing about your day-to-day realities?' Followed by 'OK, that's obviously a view you obviously feel passionate about – so please put down the hammer and tell me what I need to know ... what do we need to do better?'

Remember, when people decide of their own volition to do something then there's no stopping them. I like the lesson of the Scottish football fans who began behaving well at foreign tournaments after being praised for their good-natured party with Brazilian fans following a narrow but rather glorious defeat in a World Cup. The headlines were 'Scots in big party with Brazilians after heroic exit – hardly any arrests. (What a contrast with the English!)' Ever since then Scottish fans have made an effort to show up the English. A number of infamous incidents prior to this, in places like Rotterdam and London, illustrate just how dramatic the improvement has been.

Ironically, Manchester Council were very well aware of this mindset and reputation when they naively invited half of Glasgow along to party and spend their money in its bars at the UEFA cup final of 2008. The subsequent behaviour proved an exception to prove a rule. (The council were accused of complacency and that they didn't make proper provisions.)

Coaching, with its emphasis on discussion, thought and interaction is much more likely to induce a light bulb 'oh I see!' learning moment than a directive 'do as I say' style. This is important as we want all employees to fully understand the reasoning behind the rule or request so that they can accurately risk assess automatically on a daily basis. (Just like our SAS friend on his motorbike that we discussed on p. 16.) We want them to automatically ask the question 'what if?' Therefore as well as thinking and planning there's also an important motivational element here.

Behavioural scientists stress that the future is more emotionally motivating precisely because it hasn't happened yet. There's the energising possibility of *control*. The future is uncertain and uncertainty is exciting and sometimes frightening. We can't change the past but we can, and do, often rationalise our mistakes. When we look back we can see clearly that the mistakes of the past weren't entirely our fault and we certainly won't be repeating those mistakes in the future! It's perfectly natural but it hinders learning. When we plan to run a half marathon for charity we get excited about what we are going to do and how great it will be … often dismissing the valuable learning points from the five times we signed up in the past and failed to make the start line.

Therefore, discussing the *future* is sowing fertile mental soil if you like. It's 'pushing on an open door'. President Obama used this rather well with his positive, vague, but highly successful 'yes we can!' slogan. A good coach simply needs to add some detail to that optimism and positivity!

I remember setting up my consultancy back in the early 1990s. The adrenalin rush of early clients and planning with optimism isn't something I've come close to matching even though the consultancy has been far more successful than I'd even hoped. 'Another client! That's two now ... carry on like this and this time next year we'll have 5!' (Bruce Springsteen and many other artists have written some excellent songs about the bittersweet nature of this phenomenon!)

The idea that the future hasn't yet been written is a motivation that can be used at any time. A few months ago I tried to calm the nerves of the 55-year-old chair of a shop floor volunteer team we'd set up who was waiting to present some improvement ideas to the board of the company he worked for. His 'calming' drink had turned into *several* calming drinks ... Luckily his adrenalin levels were so high that the alcohol wasn't affecting him but he said something very interesting: 'I've never been this nervous about anything ... but it's great really. I'm loving this', and then added something hugely meaningful for the messages in this book: 'You know in 30 years with this company this is the first time I've taken any work home ... there's a thing eh?!' (When I left the hotel later to make my way home he was back at the bar but this time in the company of the German CE. They were getting on like a house on fire ... sometimes my job is hugely rewarding.)

The following section looks at some basic techniques for ensuring the coaching element of the safety talk goes well. The whole section is about encouraging the workforce to be active rather than passive in their thinking and behaviour.

COACHING BASICS – THE FEEDBACK FISH

Many supervisors need to be taught techniques for coaching. However, if you understand the principle of the 'feedback fish' you'll understand the basics of coaching. Imagine your five-year-old has brought you a picture of a fish and its pretty rubbish – just a rough outline with no detail (Figure 5.1). You'd be unlikely to say 'that's crap!' Instead, you'd probably compliment its brilliance and then hint about things that would improve it by asking questions such as 'let me think – how do fish see?' and the five-year-old will shout 'eyes!' and draw one in (Figure 5.2).

Figure 5.1   The feedback fish (first attempt)

Figure 5.2   The feedback fish (second attempt)

Though the fish is a simple, even childish, example, the analogy is very apt. Studies show that for ownership of a solution or idea to kick in, the key thing seems to be that the person being coached is the one that *says the answer first out loud*. This is true even if both people talking know full well that the 'coach' knew the answer and led them to it with questions. Of course, as with everything else in this section, using a questioning technique rather than telling is a key component of good leadership *in general*. Indeed the major principles are all generic. The most powerful coaching techniques have just as direct a relevance for safety management as they do for a management or leadership role.

When visiting a peripatetic road gang a manager might point out that they are unloading the van and setting up and yet they haven't erected barriers.

'What are you doing?! Where are the barriers?'

Alternatively, he can start a conversation about the order in which the job should be set up as per the risk assessment. What's key is that the worker has the opportunity to say something like: 'ah, that reminds me ... we're cracked on with the job here before we put the barriers up ... better put that right straight away!'

It takes a little more time but to try and model the technique itself here I'll ask the following question: which approach do you think will be most likely to impact on the workers' behaviour in the future? (Do we not *both* know the answer already?)

OWNERSHIP AND INVOLVEMENT

We mentioned the saying in Section One 'my idea had better be four times better than yours before I'll impose it on you as I know you'll work three times harder on your own idea than you will on mine'. The quality guru Deming said that 'a person most owns what they helped create'. This short section emphasises the importance of these truisms for developing a strong safety culture.

To a busy manager ownership and involvement can look very similar at a glance but in practice they aren't at all. Involvement implies asking the 'usual suspects' to ratify or comment on a decision already provisionally taken by management. (A better version of involvement is having them part of the team that takes the decision but it will almost certainly still involve the 'usual suspects'.) The problem is that whilst this process has input from the serial volunteer and naturally positive 'usual suspects' it's rarely these individuals we are seeking to influence.

Ownership involves giving the workforce itself a blank piece of paper and asking 'what do *you think*?' Inevitably, where the workforce has a good level of ownership of safety the safety culture will be strong. I don't think I've ever seen a single example that contradicts this rule.

Involvement is too often like the person at the wedding who stays silent when the vicar asks 'any person here present ...?' You're adjacent to the action and with an opportunity to get involved if you really want to. *Ownership* is introducing the couple and counselling them when last-minute nerves occur. There's an investment of creative thought and effort that is highly likely to motivate on-going monitoring, coaching and support in the process!

The analogy I personally best like is a rugby one. The difference between ownership and involvement is like being involved in a scrum in the middle of a rugby pitch. Whether the scrum is inching forwards or inching backwards looks much the same from the stands – just 16 large men arguing over the ball. However, if you're the No. 8 at the back of the scrum or the scrum half *on the pitch* who have to do something with the ball once it's won it can make all the difference in the world. The Welsh team currently have several big players (Mike Phillips and Jamie Roberts specifically) who are world class when they can work off the back of some forward momentum but of course look like ordinary big strong men when dealing with poor quality ball.

Please forgive the extended Welsh rugby analogy. There is an important learning point. How difficult is it for you to picture these players as representing potential stars in your organisation that would be hugely useful if they were 'on side' and motivated, but who look like big obstacles when not?

This absolutely reflects how nudge theory and management commitment interact. Asking 'what do *you* think?' requires more time and effort than asking 'any problems with what *I* think?' but that effort can make a huge difference to the safety culture.

REWARDING AND PRAISE ... THE POWER OF POSITIVE REINFORCEMENT

It's suggested that praise is something like 10 times as effective in changing a person's behaviour as criticism. This is because (as in Section One) we are all hot wired to be optimistic, overconfident and to learn from positive experiences. The parts of our brain that deal with positive experiences are more sensitive and powerful than the negative.

One of the very best selling management textbooks of all time, *The One Minute Manager*, includes the key slogan 'catch a person doing something *right*'. Indeed it's a key element of all 'how to' texts including the *Seven Habits of Highly Effective People*.

In order for criticism to resonate and not be seen as yet another nag it needs to have been preceded by three praises ideally. This 3:1 ratio is quoted on just about every management course. Imagine being told a month prior to an appraisal 'those two areas of weakness we discussed last year. I've noticed a significant improvement over the last 11 months and am looking forward to giving you that feedback formally next month'. What ratio of criticism would match the increase in motivation? Would it even be possible?

An interesting spot check is to ask a workforce how many instances of praise they get relative to criticism. It isn't ever 1 to 3 that's for sure! Indeed when doing our culture surveys we have a scale that ranges from 'derisory laughter' all the way through to 'no, that's not true – *never* isn't fair – I was praised once last year I think!' (I exaggerate, but not by much).

What this means in practice is that a manager needs to have a default setting as the encouraging and praising coach. That way when they do need to give some negative feedback it is far more likely to be listened to and is impactful. It's very difficult to feel that you've let someone down when their default setting is to criticise.

A word of warning is required here. Some cultures find giving praise harder than others. For example some US 'how to praise' videos really don't travel very well, especially to countries where a significant minority of the workforce can be *unhealthily* negative and cynical as well as having a *healthy* scepticism. (I've tried to have some fun with a couple of cartoons in the book and capture the real facial expressions I've often seen.)

Many training materials and techniques that work in one culture may well backfire in another. The way that praise is given is a prime example.

PRAISING THE CYNICAL WORKER

Luckily, there are several robust techniques that can be used with even the most cynical worker. One really useful example is called the 'One in Ten' technique.

The technique involves asking someone to rate themselves on a task 1 (poor) to 10 (good). When they respond with 7 perhaps, don't ask 'why only a 7!?' but instead 'Excellent, but can I ask why aren't you a 0? What do you do well?'. When they explain why they justify a 7 you listen, nod, smile, murmur and maybe even say 'sounds more like an 8 to me!' When you have built some rapport and offered some praise naturally for what they actually do well, you switch to coaching mode by asking:

> But you know I'm a safety coach and my job is to halve accidents around here. So if I can get you up from that 8 to a 9 that's my job done – well for now at least. How do you think we could do that?

I'm sure you can imagine the two people are now well primed to have a productive and constructive chat. Particularly as this approach nearly always leads naturally to 'curious why?' questions and the other objective analysis techniques that we keep stressing as vital. A few weeks ago a head of safety of a company using this exact approach told me:

> *The other day I walked past a real old school head banger (UK speak for problematic and/or foolish individual!) ... and he was actually having a constructive safety chat with one of our team. I tell you I thought well I'll be *&^%!!*

Since this chap runs a shipbuilding yard I'll argue if they can use it well *anyone* can. Indeed, it transpired that their 11 safety reps undertaking three 'One in Ten' talks a week was their *entire* behavioural safety process. I asked them if that worked for them and talked them through the five steps here ... they said 'but all the other "why?" stuff flows naturally from that anyway ...'.

The important point is that one of the problems we constantly face is that we're asked to do something that is apparently sensible and effective but because it comes straight from a textbook (or an HQ in a different country such as the United States) it isn't *appropriate* in cultures such as Europe in its original format and it goes down like a lead balloon.

I've seen plenty of examples of material being adjusted successfully to be culturally specific such as key learning from the Koran being used in the Middle East to back up training points – or a delivery style that reflects that Australians tend to like their messages as direct as possible. I don't have the space or the knowledge to suggest a list of adjustments and indeed you may need to think as much about the culture of your organisation as about the national culture when designing a programme.

One of the most famous speeches of all time, Dr Martin Luther King's 'I have a dream', is an excellent example of learning from feedback and showing flexibility as well as inspirational leadership. The key words we all remember weren't actually in the formal draft and his speech was, apparently, a bit leaden until an aide tapped his arm and whispered 'Why not try that "dream" stuff that went down so well in the church the other day?'

So some lessons on *listening* to the people around us are in there too!

There's an important generic lesson from the shipyard example and that is that we mustn't give up on a sound but rather tricky principle – in this case praise – just because of early setbacks. We must be flexible and persistent and find a better, more appropriate, way of applying it locally.

LISTENING

Listening to the workforce is vital for two reasons. One: because you might learn something. Two: because it also helps empower the person you're listening too. Here I'd like to quote perhaps the most revered modern leader of them all to connect listening, learning and leading together using the following famous example.

When locked up on Robben Island, Nelson Mandela would make a point of spending as much time as possible talking to his guards. Not just because he was trying to convert South Africa one person at a time – though of course he was – but because:

> *In genuinely listening to them I learned so much about the Boer mind-set. Their values, hopes and fears. It stood me in such good stead later when we opened formal negotiations. I had more understanding and more respect.*

And to address the second point directly – that you can influence the person you listen to by the very act of listening – we all know just how many of these guards were later in attendance at his presidential inauguration shedding tears of joy.

THE USE OF 'RATIONAL DATA' AND ILLUSTRATION

I have saved one of the best coaching techniques until last.

The numerous studies of leadership and coaching suggests that perhaps the single most effective way of changing a person's behaviour is through the use of rational data, ideally backed up with some memorable illustration. For example, we discussed the likelihood of falling down the stairs in the first chapter. For what it's worth about half of all lost time injuries (LTIs) in the offshore industry are caused by falling down the stairs (at a cost of tens of millions of pounds to the industry) but the probability of a fall being only 100,000 to 1 (or some such). This means that if a person who never holds the handrail gets lucky they might go an entire career without falling – and a supervisor has a good excuse for not making a challenge (after all a fall is unlikely on any given day and asking someone to do something as apparently mundane as holding the handrail may lead to a scornful response).

However, imagine the following conversation:

> *I've just been on a course about behavioural safety and did you know that 50% of all LTIs out here are falling down the stairs ... costs the industry about £12m annually apparently ... I wonder how many jobs that represents in the current climate?*

Pause ...

> *Only I noticed you weren't ...*

I'm sure you can imagine a conversation which would be much more likely to go well from here. The reason is simple – absolutely *no one* likes to be wrong but most of us are happy to admit that we don't know everything and are comfortable about being uninformed.

TERRORISM AND SEAT BELTS

On courses I like to ask how many people have recently challenged a taxi driver for not wearing his or her seat belt. It will be few if any who raise their hands.

We then discuss just how dangerous the roads are with reference to terrorism attacks as a benchmark. The facts are that since the attacks of 9/11 around 1,000 people have been killed by terrorists worldwide (as of 2012) but around 13 million on the roads. (The fatal road accident rate is around

1.2 million a year.) Indeed a famous example of the law of unintended consequences that links the two issues is that the year after 9/11 an *additional* 3,000 people were killed on the roads of America compared to an average year as so many people switched from air travel to the much more dangerous roads.

We then talk specifically about how many people are killed by drivers who roll their cars and end up in the back seat. Worse, when a driver is thrown about in a rolling car it's always the diagonal seat they end up in which is where most of us sit so as not to appear rude. (Sitting directly behind the driver suggests we have no intention of talking to them. So we don't often do that even if we have absolutely no intention of talking to them!)

Of that almost unimaginably large number of 1.2 million about 30,000 worldwide are killed as a consequence of being hit by a fellow passenger being flung around. This makes an un-buckled taxi driver around 330 times more dangerous to you than a terrorist (statistically speaking). At this point, we show an in-cab clip of a driver rolling his car and ending up in the back seat with some force. Even at 30mph (as in the clip) it makes for pretty spectacular viewing though it's always worth pointing out that at 60mph he'd go back with four times as much force.

We ask the audience if they will be more likely to say something next time they get in a taxi and notice the driver is unbuckled … and most hands go up. (Feedback from former delegates suggests that around 50 per cent do challenge the next driver about the seat belt. I've noticed that the majority of those that admit they didn't at least look uncomfortable about it. At least they're now clearly 'mindful' of the risk.)

The message is simple. Explain your reasoning with the use of rational data and illustrate it memorably if you can. It will maximise the chance of change.

A PERSONAL TESTIMONY – AND 'MICRO-MORTS'

In 2010, just after the Christmas break, I needed to visit a potential client in deepest British countryside in Norfolk and chose to travel there by train.

During the visit I discussed my travel options with the CEO and he asked me why I'd not driven. I explained that my decision had been influenced my knowledge of 'micro-morts'. A 'micro-mort' is basically a one in one million chance of dying in an accident. (For example, it's every 6,000 miles in a train, 230 miles on a road, six on a motorbike (180 yards on a motorbike if over the drink limit!) and so on.)

I explained I'd been up late all holiday watching the cricket in Australia and the return to work was a bit of a shock. So that whilst the early hours of the journey should be OK, as it was on a motorway, during the final two hours of driving fatigue would likely have been setting in, at pub closing time, in the dark, on Norfolk's somewhat notorious 'A' roads. Now although I'm not particularly risk averse I'd realised my micro-mort rating would go through the roof. It's worth noting that the actual risk level remained pretty good – it was the *increase* in relative risk that made me wince.

He responded that many people had told him over the years they'd considered taking the train to visit the company but then hadn't actually done so. The exception was one chap – their advanced driver coach – who apparently *always* takes the train to them! So I like to think this is a good example of user-friendly rational data helping you think like the professionals!

Let me square this whole positive feedback, 'coaching' techniques circle entirely. When this (at that time, only a *potential* client) said 'Hmm ... I'm impressed to see that you walk the talk!', what do you think it did to my likelihood of catching the train again next time?

ASSERTION – 'BUBBLES THEORY'

Finally, I'd like to suggest a mindset that can help *all* interactions go well. This technique takes advantage of the fact that we can't think and react instinctively at the same time. It has its basis in work in Transactional Analysis Interpersonal theory – which came out of California in the 1960s! The basic model is like a snowman (see Figure 5.3) with three bubbles on top of each other. The lower bubble represents passive, sulking behaviour. The top bubble represents aggressive, authoritarian or patronising behaviour. The middle bubble, however, is where you ought to be – firm, fair, *analytical* and reasonable behaviours.

You'll find that when you stop, step back and analyse yourself you'll be amazed how often you *don't* qualify for middle bubble status. Some examples:

> *Consider first the manager who closes a meeting with a challenging 'so we're all agreed? Any one got a problem with that? No? Good! Lets go then!'. This delivered with entirely rhetorical body language and voice tone! We all know that when things go wrong this person* isn't *going to say 'well it was all my*

decision, given my voice tone and body language and the way I didn't give anyone time to respond ... I mean I effectively made it impossible for anyone to object didn't I?' The delivery is very top bubble (technically 'authoritarian parent') but the consideration of it would be very much middle bubble!

The theory also talks of the 'nurturing parent'. This is still top bubble but without the aggression. The trouble is the side effects are that your paternal attitude may well be seen as patronising (because it is as you're talking down to people). This mindset will inhibit other people's development and growth and will get in the way of your listening and communication skills as you're assuming you know best. Again a strong culture needs to be based on listening, learning and mutual respect.

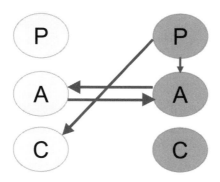

Keeping in your middle bubble by staying calm will very often lead to the other person calming down and moving into their middle bubble.

Figure 5.3   Transactional Analysis – Parent, adult or child?

For example if you've ever said to someone 'can I give you some *advice*?', even in a kindly way, you will have found that they rarely say 'yes please!' but rather automatically respond with 'no – you can bugger off!' Or maybe 'would you mind if you didn't?'. If they listen at all it will probably be grudgingly even when the advice was useful.

WHY 'BUBBLES' WORKS

There are two key factors to consider. First, *thinking* and *reacting* are mutually exclusive, so if you can train yourself to stop and think which of the three bubbles you are in then you're halfway there already. The second thing is to remember that behaviour breeds behaviour so if you're in your middle bubble other people will tend to match that. Sometimes it takes a little patience of course but it will happen more often than not. On the flip side if you're *not* in your middle bubble it's really not very easy for people around you to be in theirs because *behaviour breeds behaviour*. Aggressive responses generate aggression or sulking but pleasant objective responses usually generate similar.

The real problem is that not being in the middle bubble nearly *always* leads to problems later. Being passive means you avoid confrontation but also means people will take advantage, you'll lose respect and you will probably feel weak. Being aggressive means you might get what you want in the short term but people will resent you and get you back in some way later.

For example, I ran a course in Romania for a shipping company some years ago and we discussed how this might work. We filled a flip chart with terms such as 'withholding information', 'not helping new starts', 'boycotting social events', 'working slowly', 'looking to leave the company', 'criticising the company in the pub' and so on. At the end of this session one young officer pointed to a scar on her ear and observed: 'Or losing your head – *literally*!'

Her story was that a few months before she'd been examining a valve that had blown off and nearly taken her head with it, cutting her ear as it went. Basically someone they never caught had sabotaged it and it turned out there was a lot of bad feeling on the ship because of some very aggressive criticism that had been given to the whole crew some days before.

SUMMARY OF KEY POINTS

Finally, as a reminder of the points above here's a checklist of questions to ask the workforce, the answers to which might really help you understand how well the workforce are coached for safety:

- Ask when the last time someone walked them through a 'what if?' situation seeking to draw out their knowledge rather than simply tell them what to do.

- Ask when they were last praised for a safe act.

- Ask if that praise was given in a way that pleased them and seemed genuine.

- We can ask when the last time someone explained 'why' to them in a way that made logical sense – whether it be about a work change, a rule or some such.

- Did they use logical data? Did they try and illustrate the point with something memorable?

- How many communications are 'middle bubble' to 'middle bubble'?

AS HIS COLLEAGUES COULD TESTIFY, BOB'S COACHING STYLE LEFT A LOT TO BE DESIRED

⑥ Eliciting a Promise(?)

In this short chapter I will discuss:

- The power of eyes and 'I'.

- Reciprocity.

If the coaching techniques are done well then there is a good chance that a spontaneous commitment will be forthcoming and the need to elicit a promise will take care of itself. It's worth stressing that a promise that doesn't come from within, spontaneously, probably isn't worth having. So, if you do get a spontaneous promise then simply thank the individual concerned for it with as much warmth as you can.

That said, there will be times when – if nothing else – the *law* requires you to point out a hazard or challenge an unsafe act or situation. In this situation we do require a promise not to repeat the act/to take remedial action and if that's the case a little bit of psychology can help.

Other examples where a promise is required involve situations where a solution is 'high impact but high cost' and not likely to be addressed any time soon, if at all. This might be more complex than 'we simply haven't any money to invest'.

For example, you might find a problem with PPE compliance that is caused largely by on-going ventilation problems which themselves are caused by the design of a decrepit old building that's not really fit for current purpose. You may well find yourselves discussing a range of solutions involving portable buildings or temporary systems when someone will point out that the building is being closed in six months when everyone moves to the new buildings and the problem will be solved. Finding any meaningful amount of capital investment in this situation might prove difficult.

In which case we really do have to fight an eight-month guerrilla war as best we can, with what we have.

A SIMPLE BUT POWERFUL TIP WHEN A PROMISE *IS* NEEDED

Researchers such as Professor Robert Cialdini have found that if a person looks you in the eyes and says the 'I' word when making a promise they are something like three times less likely to go on to break that promise. You don't want them looking at the ground and mumbling 'sure, no problem ... I'm on it' or some such. That's just a grown-up version of crossing your fingers behind your back!

Imagine you're on a beach and a complete stranger asks you to look after their belongings for five minutes whilst they get their children an ice cream. If you look at them and say 'I will' how long will you keep an eye on their things? If they *never* come back for some reason would you perhaps bundle the stuff up and leave a note telling them where to find it? Your altruistic perseverance is caused by an internal 'integrity' switch which is subconsciously switched on when you (as my children say) 'pinky promise'.

To look at this from the other side, how confident would you feel about leaving your kit with someone who avoids your eyes and mumbles 'sure' in the general direction of the sea?

So when it comes to promises the 'Eyes' and the 'Is' really do have it.

RECIPROCITY

Another hugely powerful tool of social behaviour is the unwritten 'law' of reciprocity. The behaviours it encourages are hugely biologically adaptive and stem from early promises such as 'I'll take my turn to try and kill a dinosaur – you don't eat all that's left of this one when I'm gone'. It's a building block of civilisation. (Indeed, some people try and take advantage of its power. Con men and cults use this all the time by being 'nice' or by giving free gifts and trying to oblige us to do something for them in return. It's why we get sent free pens by charities.)

Some studies suggest that this 'fairness' concept is the most powerful of all social concepts and popular culture provides any number of examples of its appeal. Marlon Brando's 'Godfather' and nearly every character played by Clint Eastwood or Charles Bronson would fall into the 'harsh but *fair*' and thus admirable category. We curse when we are unlucky – but we positively *seethe* when we are treated *unfairly*.

It helps explain why a workforce can spend years getting over an initiative that was launched but not followed through even though a lot of workforce time and effort was put into it. (Have you ever heard a workforce refer to 'another initiative' without inserting an oath in the middle?)

It is an excellent idea to always ask ourselves 'if I was in their shoes would I think this unfair?' In the face of what appears unreasonable indifference or cynicism it's always worth asking if any unfairness is perceived – either at the time or previously.

With reference to the design solutions we discussed earlier in the book the very best form of reciprocity is when we can say 'if we get these suggestions implemented by the end of the month will you come up with some more please?'

After all, that seems fair.

SUMMARY OF KEY POINTS

- A promise made to the floor is three times as likely to be broken as an 'I' promise made whilst looking you in the eye. If you need someone to make you a promise make sure it's a 'promise promise'!

- Reciprocity is a hugely powerful cause of behaviour. A perception of unfairness very often explains what can seem unreasonably negative behaviour. More positively it can often lead to a 'virtuous circle'.

BOB'S ATTEMPTS AT SINCERE PRAISE WERE STILL
CONSIDERED A LITTLE OVER THE TOP IN THE FOUNDRY

(7) Close Out

In this chapter I will discuss:

- Sincere thanks.

- SMART actions.

- Closing the loop.

As ever, follow up is perhaps the most important section of all because if you get your follow up wrong much of what was right will be undone. Yet there are really only a few things to remember.

SINCERE THANKS

Remember to say 'thank you' for anything at all sensible that comes out of the discussion. Thank the person warmly and sincerely too. As we've discussed, 85 per cent of a communication isn't in what we say it's about how we say it. If you're going through the motions, they'll know you are insincere. On the other hand a sincere thank you reinforces anything positive and makes it more likely next time.

You might even like to use Bill Clinton's trick of making some sort of physical touch to add emphasis. Apparently how sincere he was trying to *appear to be* followed this system:

- warm handshake ...

- warm handshake with left hand clasped over joined hands ...

- warm handshake with left hand clasped about forearm ...

- warm handshake with left hand clasped on shoulder.

Some commentators said it correlated with how big a lie he was telling and that the more 'sincerity' he put into it the bigger the lie, but that's sheer cynicism! I'm sure you get the point. Whether Bill Clinton was telling the truth in every case his 'touchy' approach worked very well for him!

I must stress the need to use this technique appropriately and in a culturally sensitive manner. Anyone who's ever played sport knows that the slightest nod of the head in acknowledgement for something well done from the strong but silent 'hard man' of the team can make you feel six inches taller.

The point is to let the person know you appreciate it as sincerely as you can. Don't go through the motions or blindly copy someone else. Just make an effort and be sincere.

WHERE THE LEARNING REQUIRES A PLAN OF ACTION

Ideally any agreements here will follow the famous SMART acronym:

- Specific

- Measurable

- Agreed

- Realistic

- Time set

The idea of the acronym is to make a realistic plan that is clear, specific and can be followed. One of the very first design solutions I saw was at a chemical company where people would 'quickly nip in' to a high hazard area to check the reading on a gauge just inside a door without donning the required PPE. The job that only took a few seconds but donning the extensive PPE required several minutes.

The very simple action plan was:

> *Get maintenance to confirm that the gauge can be moved to the outside wall. It shouldn't take more than an hour to do that. Pete, you make sure they have the required PPE now so that ideally they scope the job today and get this done tomorrow. There shouldn't be a problem as they are in the middle of an on-going planned maintenance programme and I will*

add a half a day to that. Let me know by tomorrow lunchtime if there are any problems I haven't thought of and ask them to let me know in Friday's review meeting at the latest that it's done or the reason why it hasn't if it hasn't.

Or arrange for it to be implemented if you can't delegate directly like this. However, do follow up with the person you delegated to ask 'Did you sort out X and did you get back to Y afterwards to let them know how it turned out?' Unless it's all affirmative don't let it go. The final chance to demonstrate your genuine commitment to safety excellence is by your persistence here.

Then let the person know what you've done and say thank you (again). Then get their picture in an in-house magazine … (or some such!).

GETTING BACK TO SOMEONE

The third technique is simple to describe but harder to do. If you say you'll follow something up and let someone know how that goes then you *have to do so*. Even a simple message such as 'it seems it's a lot more complicated when you get into it than it looks' is better than 'sweet … *nothing*'.

A BEST PRACTICE INVESTMENT

A PERSON WHOSE JOB IS TO COVER ALL THE WEAKNESSES

As we've made clear several times above, knowledge itself is no use at all if we don't make use of it. Feedback and communication is key to this process. We really don't care *how* a company does the things above or *who* does it – in good behavioural tradition we just care that it gets done, gets done well and gets done quickly.

I'd like to suggest a role that can be done part-time (or even full-time in a big company) and that directly address the several major weaknesses we often see compromising the benefits of a good approach to safety.

We recommend that some of the workforce be trained up as behavioural safety/human error champions. They'll need to understand the basics of human error and this will require a few days of training. They will also require a senior manager mentor who can clear blockages and write cheques. Once trained and empowered their task is to:

- Be the first point of call for any ideas and suggestions that come out of a safety contact (to make it easy for the supervisor or manager).

- Be the first point of call for any worker who has an idea – just after a safety contact has taken place (or at any other time).

- Tell people what's happening and why. Not just verbally but via noticeboards and other media that all can see.

- Get back to anyone who was involved in making changes or improvements in the system to let them know what's happening or at least explaining why if nothing seems to be happening.

- Be consulted whenever a change occurs – even if the change is not anticipated to have a safety impact. (Or perhaps especially when it's not considered to have a safety impact.)

- Look at the hiring process from a safety perspective.

- Look at supplier selection and contracting from the same point of view.

- Be involved in the purchasing of equipment.

And also:

- Running (or at least helping with) the on-going *process* safety audits.

- Running an on-going follow up audit of the safety leadership behaviours requested above.

You might like to think of them as the sweeper of 'unintended consequences'.

It's a simple idea. This role takes the inconvenience out of the process whenever possible to bridge the gap between good intentions and actions. Remember, designing out inconvenience proactively is always a good idea.

SUMMARY OF KEY POINTS

- Make sure to thank anyone involved sincerely to show genuine gratitude for their input and also to help embed the behaviour.

- Make sure that plans are SMART – avoid vague instructions that allow a little 'wriggle room'.

- Follow up to ensure the plan was followed and give feedback as appropriate!

- If feasible train up a dedicated individual whose job is to proactively address these points.

Conclusion

These safety talks are pretty simple. What you are trying to do is to communicate clearly the standards you expect and to throw an appropriate leadership shadow to inspire safer behaviour by setting an example, empowering and coaching. You are trying to learn why things aren't perfect and to show your *genuine* commitment by applying those lessons whenever that's financially or logistically viable.

At the start of the book I suggested that we get the health and safety standards we are prepared to accept and that we communicate this with our leadership over and above compliance and process integrity.

By being out there talking about safety and using the information and learning you demonstrate your commitment. By leading properly you inspire 'willing followers' and by working from a 'Just Culture' perspective you enhance trust and fairness and learn how best to use your resources.

It's very much easier said than done of course – but it really isn't rocket science.

Appendix 1
Final Checklist

The following questions are provided as a simple reminder of the key points. If you are able to answer yes to the majority of them after a safety conversation then I *guarantee* you'll have laid another brick in the wall of a strong safety culture.

- Were you able to get the person talking to you in a reasonably relaxed and natural way?

- Did it remain professional and focused and not overly 'matey'?

- Did you ask 'why?' *curiously* about any issues seen or raised?

- Did you proactively ask 'anything slow, uncomfortable or inconvenient?' about doing the job safely?

- Were you able to praise something you saw? Or praise came naturally because you used the 'rate yourself 1 to 10' approach?

- Did you use a questioning coaching technique to get them to be the one to come up with the answer and to consider 'what if?' situations?

- Were any promises made to you inclusive of the 'I' word whilst looking you in the eye and just after you promised to do something for them?

- Were any actions agreed SMART?

- Finally, do you agree that whether we're talking about following up SMART actions delegated, actions you've committed to yourself – or just getting out and undertaking a safety talk at all. RUDE NIKE RULES ALWAYS APPLY!

Appendix 2
Suggested Basic Six-Items Checklist

1. **How do you rate your supervisor's praise and feedback?**

    5 Often praises routine safe behaviour

    4

    3 Rarely praises safe behaviour/praises only exceptional behaviour

    2

    1 Never praises safe behaviour

2. **How often does your supervisor coach rather than tell?**

    5 Coaches by drawing out knowledge and options whenever feasible

    4

3 Sometimes coaches by using questions rather than telling

2

1 Never uses questioning or coaching techniques

3. How often does your supervisor lead by example?

5 Always leads by example

4

3 Usually leads by example

2

1 Sometimes leads by example

4. How often does your supervisor involve and empower?

5 Involves and empowers in design and decision making whenever viable

4

3 Has involved and empowered but also frequently misses chances to do so

2

1 Rarely if ever involves the workforce in design and decision making

5. How well does your supervisor learn about improvement opportunities?

5 Always asks 'curious why' and often asks 'anything slow or uncomfortable' questions

4

3 Often asks 'curious why' and sometimes asks 'anything slow or uncomfortable' questions

2

1 Rarely asks 'why' curiously

6. How well does your supervisor follow up and close out safety actions?

5 Always follows up and ensures close out – or communicates reasons for any delay

4

3 Quite good at following up and closing out safety related actions

2

1 Poor at following up and closing out safety actions

This basic list could, of course, be several times longer and more precisely behaviourally anchored. However, even with something this simple, if you systemically follow up these items so that an average score of, for example, 3.1 can be turned into a score of 3.9 that will, most definitely, reflect a transformation in your safety culture.

References and Further Reading

Broadbent, D.G. (2007) 'What Kind of Safety Leader are You?' Paper presented at the National Health and Safety Conference, Auckland, New Zealand.

Daniels, A. and Agnew, J. (2010) *Safe by Accident?* Atlanta: Performance Management Publications.

Dekker, S. (2008) *The Field Guide to Understanding Human Error*, Farnham: Ashgate.

Geller, E.S. (2001) *The Psychology of Safety Handbook*, Florida: CRC Press.

Goldstein, N.J., Martin, S.J. and Cialdini, R.B. (2007) *Yes! 50 Secrets of Persuasion*, London: Profile Books.

Heinrich, H.W. (1959) *Industrial Accident Prevention: A Scientific Approach* (4th edn), New York: McGraw-Hill.

Hopkins, A. (2008) *Failure to Learn*, Sydney: CCH Australia.

Mandela, N. (1994) *Long Walk to Freedom*, London: Abacus.

Reason, J. (1997) *Managing the Risks of Organisational Accidents*, Farnham: Ashgate.

Reason, J. (2008) *The Human Contribution*, Farnham: Ashgate.

Thaler, R.H. and Sunstein, C.R. (2009) *Nudge*, London: Penguin.

Vroom, V. (1992) *Management and Motivation*, London: Penguin.

If you find the material in this book of interest can I recommend the following readable books – for a long journey or perhaps as the 'one non-fiction one' to be taken on holiday! None are directly referenced in the text but were in mind every time I mentioned 'unintended consequences' or 'why people do what they do'!

Berne, E. (1964) *Games People Play (Transactional Analysis)*, London: Penguin.

Brown, D. (2007) *Tricks of the Mind*, London: 4 Books.

Gladwell, M. (2002) *The Tipping Point*, London: Penguin.

Gladwell, M. (2005) *Blink*, London: Penguin.

Hallinan, J.T. (2009) *Why We Make Mistakes*, New York: Broadway Books.

Levitt, S. and Dunbar, S. (2007) *Freakonomics*, London: Penguin.

Levitt, S. and Dunbar, S. (2010) *Superfreakonomics*, London: Penguin.

McFarlin, B. (2004) *Drop the Pink Elephant*, Chichester: Capstone.

If you have found this book useful you may be interested in other titles from Gower

The Human Contribution:
Unsafe Acts, Accidents and Heroic Recoveries
James Reason
Hardback: 978-0-7546-7400-9
Paperback: 978-0-7546-7402-3

Behind Human Error
David D. Woods, Sidney Dekker, Richard Cook,
Leila Johannesen, and Nadine Sarter
Hardback: 978-0-7546-7833-5
Paperback: 978-0-7546-7834-2
ebook: 978-0-7546-9650-6

Addiction at Work:
Tackling Drug Use and Misuse in the Workplace
Edited by Hamid Ghodse
Hardback: 978-0-566-08619-9

Innovative Thinking in Risk, Crisis,
and Disaster Management
Edited by Simon Bennett
Hardback: 978-1-4094-1194-9
ebook: 978-1-4094-1195-6

A Short Guide to Operational Risk
David Tattam
Paperback: 978-0-566-09183-4
ebook: 978-1-4094-2891-6

Just Culture: Balancing Safety and Accountability
Sidney Dekker
Hardbck: 978-1-4094-4061-1
Paperback: 978-1-4094-4060-4
ebook: 978-1-4094-4062-8

Occupational Health and Safety
Edited by Ronald J. Burke, Sharon Clarke and Cary L. Cooper
Hardback: 978-0-566-08983-1
ebook: 978-1-4094-3207-4

Safety Culture:
Assessing and Changing the Behaviour of Organisations
John Bernard Taylor
Hardback: 978-1-4094-0127-8
ebook: 978-1-4094-0128-5

Visit **www.gowerpublishing.com** and

- search the entire catalogue of Gower books in print
- order titles online at 10% discount
- take advantage of special offers
- sign up for our monthly e-mail update service
- download free sample chapters from all recent titles
- download or order our catalogue